The Te

(a week and a half and over thirty years to know him)

by Sue Parsons

Cover: Haida blanket box, hammered copper on cedar.

The Tenth Night

Copyright 2012 by Sue Parsons

Parsons, Sue

ISBN: 978-0-692-01670-1

Library of Congress Control Number: 2012932830

Printed in the United States of America

Treehugger Press
112 Windward Drive, Bellingham, WA 98229
thermojeff@yahoo.com

Available at Village Books, Bellingham, WA

An Invitation to My Muse

You appear to me
As the statue of David
Smooth, carved white musculature
The perfection of youth

You gaze at me askance
Your thoughts elsewhere
Not unlike mine
When I sit down to write

Maybe the artpiece you should show yourself as
Is the extended hand of God in the fresco
The artist's name is the same
But the message is certainly different

Please turn your full attention here, on me
Let me create something beautiful and enduring
Help me reach inside, grasp the truth
And pour it onto this keyboard

MANY THANKS:

My family, especially Shauna, Jeremie, Jeff, Ward, Brad and Donna, Bill and Gloria. I would not have lasted an hour without your reassuring presence, shoulders both for tears and muscle, and for giving me a reason to continue.

Friends at Marshall School and in the neighborhood, most especially Robin, for their steadfast support.

Fellow authors from memoir writing classes and my own Friendly Writers for their inspiration.

Nancy Aronie for the freedom to write the truth.

And to the fandom geeks of real and invented name – May the Force be with you – always.

Dedicated to my husband, Jeff Parsons, without whom two Parsons generations would not exist, and neither would I in the form I have come to be.

The First Night

"I think I'm in trouble."

He is standing in the den doorway, a little hunched, pale and somewhat anxious-looking. A few moments before he was up in the hobby room, working on some model or other. Now he just...doesn't look right. He is rarely very expressive, so over the years I have learned to glean a lot of information from small changes. Is this about finances, his job?

AIM conversation and dinner plans forgotten, I swivel in my desk chair and gesture to his. "Sit down. What's wrong?"

He slowly fingers his upper shoulders. His silver hair is askew. He sits in his office chair gingerly, his back and neck rigid. "I don't know. My neck is really stiff. This is the worst headache I've ever had."

This from a man who rarely complains. He has my full attention. He was working in the garden earlier. Is he having an allergic reaction to some chemical he used?

Clearly uneasy in the computer chair, he stands up again.

"Would you be more comfortable lying down?" I wonder.

"Maybe," he agrees, and starts back out the door down the hall to our bedroom. I follow right behind, beginning to worry if he is going to stumble or pass out. While he is not staggering, he certainly doesn't look all that steady on his feet. It is as if he is measuring each step.

We make it to the bedroom, and he tentatively lowers himself onto his back. Within an instant, he is sitting up and rolling off the bed. "No, THAT isn't gonna work..." he says with finality.

"Maybe sort of semi-tilted? Like in the recliner?"

"Could help." I trail him back down the hall out to the family room corner where the old tan corduroy chair lives. He sits down slowly and attempts to get comfortable while keeping his upper body stiff. "This isn't good."

Sitting down on the couch opposite him, I try to think of what to offer him. I know he won't take any analgesics, convinced he is allergic. That one episode of facial swelling after aspirin, despite medical test results concluding no allergy, made him shy away from all pain medications. He has toughed out sciatica attacks on his own. Won't take anything for a cold or cough, like that horrible one he had the last couple of weeks. Doesn't consult a doctor or even go in for regular checkups unless required for a Boy Scout adventure hike. And now that our son has gotten his Eagle, those outings are over, too, and so is the checkup routine.

"Can I get you anything? Should I massage…?"

"Oh, no," he declines, instantly rejecting the notion of my touching him. The way he says it convinces me of the level of discomfort he must be in. "I feel a little nauseated."

After a few minutes of watching him trying to cope with the pain, gritting his teeth and hissing when he attempts to move his head, I finally ask the impossible. "Do I need to take you somewhere? Get some help?"

I am dumbstruck when he assents. He rises from the chair and says, "Yeah. Maybe." He seems as bewildered as I am.

That means the same as, GOD YES GET ME SOME HELP! from a normal person.

I move to stand behind him as he slowly walks past me, and I measure my steps to match his, my arms haloing his without touching, ready to slow his fall if he tumbles.

We pass through the dining room and have just made it into the living area when he speaks again. "No. They are coming to me." With all deliberateness, he lowers one knee to the floor, gripping the side of the leather couch, drops the other knee, then very slowly rolls to his side, then his back. Resting his hands on his chest, he waits for me to get it.

"Oh!" I mutter, then run down the hall back to the den where the portable phone is. Grabbing it with now shaking hands, I punch in the numbers and give what information I can to the dispatcher. "Male. Age 58. Very sudden, horrible headache, nausea, a little dizzy, can't get comfortable." I finally voice the unthinkable. "Might be a heart attack, a stroke...?" The dispatcher takes down the information and tells me to make sure to unlock the door and be ready to direct the rescue team to where my husband is.

I bring the phone back out to the living room and throw open the front door. Jeff has rolled to his side and is retching a little. "Think I'm gonna lose it..."

Racing to the kitchen, I grab a metal bowl and a towel and return to his side. I am trying to comfort him, but recall that he didn't want me to touch his neck or shoulders, so I stick to his sides, chest, and legs. I remind him that, on the emergency shows, they always say to loosen clothing and remove belts. He takes his off, lifting his lower torso off the floor by pressing down with his feet, and then unbuttons his jeans. I open his shirt a bit, saying reassuring words I don't believe. These kinds of things don't happen to us, right? This is the type of thing you read about in a book or watch on a bad made-for-TV movie.

It seems that an awful lot of minutes pass before help arrives. In reality, the paramedics come quickly, and I beckon them in and get out of the way. I offer the little bit of information I have as they begin to talk to Jeff and attach monitors and IVs. They are asking him questions about his neck swelling and if his facial features had gotten saggy, which he is denying. I insert that, as a matter of fact, that was what I saw – why his face didn't look right. I try to tell them about his problem with needles; they are asking him something, and suddenly he is not with them.

"Mr. Parsons? Mr. Parsons?"

"He can't..." I reply. "He's passed out..."

At first I assume that needle insertion caused Jeff's common vascular response of faintness, but then my world comes to a jarring halt as my husband's body seizes. Animalistic groans, gas passing, all of his usually ever-present control evaporates, and the men pull out equipment and spread out mysterious packages on the floor as one of them squawks information into a radio; I stand and walk out the still-open door.

I stride into a clot of neighbors who were summoned by the sirens and the presence of crisis vehicles in their territory. Robin, my next-door neighbor for over three decades, has already figured out who this is about and just nods when I say, "It's Jeff." Not even fifteen minutes have passed since he climbed down the stairs from working on his ship model.

Jeff and I bought our first house in Chino, California. That's in the Southern half of the state, around forty miles east of Los Angeles, in an area called The Inland Empire. We had no emperor, however. In terms of terrain, ours was on the edge of a gigantic bowl, the lips of which were the San Gabriel Mountains to the northwest, the San Bernardino Mountains to the north and northeast, trailing down a bit to the east, and Chino Hills to the south. Below that is Orange County. Chino is also right next to Los Angeles County to the northwest, and is barely within San Bernardino County. Riverside County is off to the southeast. So our empire was within striking distance of several others, but no incursions occurred while I was living there.

It was 1974, and Jeff and I had been searching for a home we could buy. The little home we rented in Anaheim was not in a great neighborhood, and throwing one's money away on rent is never a good idea if you can afford to buy. Our budget was around $25,000, which would have us paying around $215 a month for a mortgage and homeowner's insurance. Jeff's father, Howard, would be fronting us for the ten percent down payment, and we were going to be paying him back a little each month. These payments would be kept in a ledger and considered a bank loan, with all of the attendant scrutiny and timeliness.

Our search encompassed a large geographical area, but was limited in terms of supply. Most of the older homes we saw were in foreclosure, and in bad condition. With a small child, and me with no expertise in handymanship, most of the repair work would have fallen to Jeff. We decided to keep looking.

The range of our hunt widened. From Hacienda and Rowland Heights to Corona we found neighborhoods on the downswing. Diamond Bar proved to be expensive or with houses in similar condition to the foreclosures. Carbon Canyon, due to the narrow water pipes, was iffy as to whether we could get an FHA loan there, although there were a couple of cute houses we liked. Finally, we went beyond the end of Carbon Canyon Road to the unknown edges of Los Angeles County – Pomona – and San Bernardino County – Chino, Ontario and Montclair.

In the corner bordered by those two counties were several brand-new housing developments. Over the course of a couple of weekends Jeff and I looked at four of them. Nestled among orange groves and egg ranches, some unlandscaped dirt lots provided the basis for rows of closely-spaced homes, perhaps four dozen per tract. We looked through the model homes and examined which houses remained to be selected. The development we scrutinized in Montclair, Spacemaster Homes, had a quirky method of studding. They had used I-beams. That put Jeff off, somewhat. Also, the Ontario-Montclair schools didn't have quite the track record for student achievement that Chino schools did. So we traveled further south, to Chino, and began to look at the remaining newer developments there.

Towards the end of the day we hit a small group of houses sited on land which had formerly been a cow pasture owned by a family whose home anchored the development. The Elrods now owned a meat-packing shop a block away. Their older home occupied an acre of land peppered by fruit trees and outbuildings as well as a large swimming pool in the backyard. The couple had two children who had started families of their own, one having bought one of the homes in the development. We checked out the model homes and were informed that only four houses remained for sale. As we stood in the model, one of the homes down the street got a buyer.

Quickly we scanned those that were still on the market. Jeff found some foundation cracks in two of them, so back we went to the model home, one with gold shag carpet and four bedrooms, a long ranch design with a double garage. Our toddler daughter Shauna ran up and down the hallway, delighted with all the open space. That sold it for us.

This was a scary, exhilarating time. Relying only on Jeff's income at Unocal, we were buying a home. The house payment was nearly sixty dollars a month more than the rent we had been paying in Anaheim, and now we would be spending money on landscape, fencing, window treatments and the like. And Jeff would have a longer commute – driving through Carbon Canyon to Placentia to get to work. I would also have to drive a greater distance to get to my college classes. We were farther away from family, and knew no one in this new area. Stores, doctors, dentists, everything would be different. It was even somewhat hotter in the summers, due to the greater distance from the ocean and its afternoon breezes.

We would have a lot of adjusting to do. But I had never imagined we could afford to purchase a four bedroom house this soon in our young marriage.

I got down to the business of moving in – putting in shelf paper and arranging the kitchen, getting our bedrooms, closets and bathrooms squared away. Shauna "helped" as well as a sixteen-month old can. We had a lot of empty space initially, with one bedroom and a den unfurnished. Jeff reveled in his spacious garage – all his. For three people, it was a big house of 1250 square feet. The front of the house looked out on the Elrod's home, which was a pleasant thing to look at. Our backyard ended in a ditch over which a block wall loomed. The wall belonged to the church on the other side of it, so if we wanted to fill in the space we would have to erect a retaining wall.

Across the street on the west side was a ranchette and just south of that was an egg ranch owned by an older Russian couple who spoke little English. Further down the street was an orange grove on the west side, with ranchettes on the east side of the street. Down at the corner was the elementary school our children would attend. Less than a mile away was a grocery store and a few small shops.

At first we thought having a church for a neighbor would be great! Hardly any noise, not much traffic…and then we lived through our first hot Sunday. We had to open most of our *windows that night to catch the bit of breeze. The churchgoers had to open their windows early in the morning due to the heat buildup during the week.*

They liked to sing. A lot. Early every Sunday morning. They also practiced late every Wednesday evening, then were very excited slamming car doors in the parking lot, with their kids running around hooting and hollering. A church is a quiet neighbor? Not so much.

After moving in during a drizzly, blessedly cool day in early June, we stepped out and began meeting our new neighbors. We had already heard one, just across the street, the older gentleman former rancher, now the proprietor of the nearby meat market, his herd having been sold from the walnut tree peppered pastures our houses now sprouted on. Cecil was a whistler, much like my dad, but not quite so accomplished nor lyrical. Still, there was a sense of familiarity there that I found comforting.

Flanking us on the right as we looked out to the street, we had another older man who announced his presence with aromatic cigar smoke. A skinny, wiry man, he possessed a wife, Cookie, he occasionally verbally abused. I heard the wife go off only once, and that was at her nearly teenage son, who had been caught stealing. Listening to her, we secretly rejoiced that she would be so appropriately outraged, and hoped it would make a difference in the boy's behavior. Most unfortunately, as we discovered many years later, it didn't.

One house further down the street were the Ramirezes- an imposing father, friendly mother, two daughters and a son. The children attended Catholic school; they alternately got along with and were estranged from us. I wish I had gotten to know the mom better; within a decade cancer had claimed her.

A young couple and their dog occupied the house just west of us. They must have worked long hours; I hardly recall seeing them outside at all. They lasted less than a year. With the breakup of their marriage their house was sold to the Emerys, a couple slightly younger than us with a baby daughter. Robin, the mom, wound up being my great friend.

Over on the far west corner, however, was the caretaker of us all: Mrs. Lopez. I learned her first name some years after moving in. Jennie swept the curbs all the way to the other end of the street, worried that cars would slip on the damp sycamore leaves that periodically blew over from the Elrods'. She lived alone, having lost her husband and son before we ever moved in. I returned to the neighborhood last year in the fall; despite my pointing to my old house and explaining I had lived there for over thirty years, Mrs. Lopez had lost that part of her life.

At some point I walk back into the house and notice that the emergency team is inserting a tube in Jeff's nose, perhaps trying to get some medication into him. I turn around and stumble back out the doorway.

It is just after six o'clock on a nice Spring Saturday evening. Families all over Chino are sitting down to dinner and arguing over TV shows. Soccer games are breaking up in the park and deferring to bar-be-ques. Kids are whining to get their parents to let them play outside just a little longer. My husband's paramedic entourage is wheeling him out on a gurney to the back of the waiting ambulance at the end of the driveway, positioning IV bags and monitoring equipment around him. As they get further information from the local hospital, I notice that he is grimacing and posturing. Brain damage....

All at once everything changes. One of the attendants is telling me that a helicopter is meeting them at the park across the street. Chino Medical Center does not have adequate staff to handle what is probably a large bleedout in Jeff's brain. It's a stroke. He will be airlifted to Arrowhead Medical in Colton – perhaps a 45-minute drive away. The helicopter will make it in less than 10. "You can drive over and meet us there in emergency," he says, and off they go to the park.

I have to call Jeffy, I realize. Our son is at work at an ice cream shop in the town south of us. Then, immediately, I worry. He will be driving back here like a nineteen-year-old boy whose dad was having a stroke.

So I return to the house, walk past the blood on the carpet and call him; repeatedly I order him not to get into an accident on the way here. I know I call some other people. Who? I glance at my computer screen and notice that the chat I had been in is still active. I had been speaking with an online buddy I had never met – a fellow Star Wars fan who who is a dispatcher for the police department in a little town in Vermont. Opening the chat window one more time, I type "Jeff – heart attack or stroke. Pray." Hitting "send", I shut down the computer, lock up the house and go back out onto the front lawn.

Meanwhile, Robin is getting ready to take us over to the hospital in her van. It is probably a very good idea for me not to try driving this distance to an unfamiliar location right now. We'll work out details about how to get back later.

The helicopter arrives at the park. It seems to take forever before they finally lift off again. This is my husband's first helicopter ride. I am thinking that I really hope he isn't conscious for it, but geez, what if this is the only one he ever takes? A few years ago I gave him a WarBird ride gift certificate for Christmas so that he could co-pilot an old WWII bomber. He had been fascinated with the whole concept. Here we have another first for him, and he will probably not recall any of it.

My son arrives within five minutes, careening around the corner and slamming to a stop in front of our house in a cloud of dust. I try not to comment on the manner in which he got here, nor the velocity involved. I can tell he is very tense and that any attempts to calm or soothe him will no doubt be met with resistance. Into Robin's van we go. I am hoping, since it is a Saturday evening, there won't be too much traffic on the freeway.

 I am shell-shocked, as though I am coming out of a concussed state, as we travel to the hospital. I try to fill my son in as much as I can, and Robin's brain must be racing as she makes suggestions about phone calls and family preparations. You hear about people describing an event as surreal; we are in a place where time and thought are very fluid and abruptly tangential. Jeff. The future. Parents. Kids. My class.

Among my students that year are several special needs kids. Some are on meds, some are pulled out for other resources and services. Much prep work is required to arrange for the various academic needs within that one room. Many kids are fragile. The administrators and office staff are always ready to act upon my alerting them to the need to immediately remove one of my children from the classroom, whereupon his Mom would dash across the street to help calm him. In short, it is going to be very difficult for another teacher to step into that room with little preparation and make things come together for those children. So I worry that the right person I have in mind might not be available to take over.

Our daughter Jeremie is more than eight months pregnant. How might this event with her dad affect her health and that of her baby?

At what point should I alert Jeff's parents and mine? Should I wait until something definite was diagnosed, or let everyone know right away that something catastrophic was on the way?

Shauna will want to come down from Washington, but she has the kids to deal with, and both she and Ward have jobs. When to call?

If Jeff survives this, will he be able to talk or move? I can absolutely help him with therapies or lifestyle changes, so I will need to take some time off work. He will definitely have to stop working for at least a little while. Forever?

14

WILL he survive this? When I saw him in the back of the ambulance, was that the last time I would see him alive?

I call people. Robin is coaching, always the voice of reason, the person to have around in case of an emergency.

Robin was my very first neighbor friend. At first, both of us were busy with our respective little ones, but the ice was broken when I caught her toddler daughter having slipped out front. I herded her to her door and called for backup. Robin, ever jovial and quick-thinking, jumped out onto the porch, gaffled up her baby and invited me in for coffee.

At that point in my life, I was not so great at making or maintaining friendships. I always remained somewhat aloof and distant. However, Robin wasn't having that. She blustered her way through my defenses and told jokes until I broke, sometimes literally into helpless hysterics.

We each had another daughter within months of each other, joined the PTA at the elementary school down the street and got involved with classroom help and volunteering. I read Family Circle and National Geographic; she videotaped endless TV shows and read romance novels. One day we laughed until we cried reading the back covers of her paperbacks, inventing more and more outlandish names for the characters and throwing them into ever more improbable situations. Shopping together, especially in the open air market known as the Chino Auction, was a common event for us. Using the old Chevy truck with the hydraulic lift gate my dad had bequeathed to Jeff and me, we would throw all manner of debris in the back and head off to the dump with a few kids strapped together in the long front seat, as I struggled to find enough room to operate the stick shift on the steering column. Once we threw all of the kids in her Dragon Wagon and headed off to Gemco for grocery shopping. It was close to 100 degrees and humid that day, there was no AC in the car, and after we had loaded all our purchases into the trunk the car refused to start. So when we finally got home, we threw the kids in her backyard above-ground pool, and she excused herself to answer the phone, which wound up being an obscene call we would guffaw about for years. The poor man on the line, struggling to maintain his pseudo-sexy raspy voice, but unable to be heard above the children squealing in the pool, finally had to resort to shouting in order for Robin to hear his urgent message – "I want…to sniff… YOUR PANTIES!"

With husbands who were less than swift in the romance department, we decided to celebrate one another's birthdays. One October, I found what I considered a pretty spiffy autumn gift bag, and enclosed what was probably a book-lovers shirt inside. That following December I got the bag back with no doubt a sweater. Folding the bag and tissue carefully, I waited out the ten months to regift it, adding a tacky rose-shaped beige bow. Yes, it went back in my closet two months later. The running gag gift bag continued even after I moved a thousand miles away.

For over twenty-five years we ran Marshall Elementary School PTA, even after our own children had all graduated from elementary school. We took turns being secretary, president, treasurer and nearly every other officer on the docket. By that time both of us worked at the school; she was the librarian and I was a first grade teacher. Robin and I were always *on school planning teams, throwing ourselves into making our neighborhood school the best it could be. For over two decades we worked, volunteered, played and cried together. But mostly I remember the laughter. When Robin laughed, no one could stay serious for long.*

Once we arrive at the medical center, we check in to let the hospital personnel know we are there, and that Jeff is no doubt already being examined. Then the wait begins.

Jeffy has issues with that. He paces outside the waiting room. Robin sits with me, occasionally questioning the workers there as to Jeff's situation. She finds it hard to believe that I can be so calm and acquiescent, willing to wait until people come to me to inform me of his condition. She would have ranted and raved and thrown tantrums, insisting on seeing him, if it were her loved one. Part of the reason for my reticence is lifelong submission to authority, part is the "no news is good news" philosophy. I go out and commune with Jeffy and call my brother and his wife.

Bill and Gloria leave a church charity event and arrive very quickly, still wearing their T-shirts from the affair. We discuss how and when the news should be broken to our parents, whose health is fragile and who were born worriers. After assuring my brother I would call our folks as soon as I had any news, I convince them to go on home, as by now it is getting quite late. Robin also leaves, taking my son with her so that when he returns we will have a car to go back and forth.

On a visit from Washington, I spent the day with my brother, Bill, and his wonderful wife, Gloria. Interspersed with the catchings-up on family, relative weather patterns of California versus Washington and musings on grandchildren, there were moments of reminiscence. While munching on breakfast out, sipping water at their home, touring an old restored Victorian house near their house, or dining out, there were bits and pieces of our folks. Just before I left to return to my brother-in-law's place in Placentia, Gloria rushed into the den and brought out a few slips of paper she said she had found among my parents' keepsakes. They were letters I had written to my parents; one to my dad Father's Day when Shauna was still an only, and the other to my mom on the occasion of their anniversary almost twenty years later. I was very glad Gloria had saved these for me.

For Dad, I had written…

> *This is the one day when we reach for all the lofty terms*
> *To tell you of the man we see when we think of "Dad".*
> *This is not your average over-fifty guy. He doesn't look like a "grandpa" – more like a seasoned athlete, a retired football pro.*
>
> *But inside this strong, powerful body is the heart of a modern-day St. Francis a gentle man with the love of both nature and his fellow man, but especially of his wife. Always with a ready smile, a joke, a wave.*
>
> *This is a man we not only love and respect as a father, but also like and enjoy as a person.*
>
> *Have a nice day, Dad. We like you more each day we spend with you.*
>
>
> *Love, your kids*
> *Bill, Gloria, and Josef, Sue, Jeff, and Shauna*

To the end of his life, Dad never looked his age. I had always wondered if perhaps there was someone of Native American ancestry in his lineage. His hair remained a deep dark brown with peppery accents and was lush and wavy.

The St. Francis mentioning refers to Dad's uncanny ability to attract wildlife. Wild birds would listen to his melodic whistling and occasionally perch on his outstretched finger.

And his love for my mother was unlike any I had ever known. He fell in love with her on sight and was completely helpless without her.

And Mom's note went like this:

Dear Mom,

This evening I had the pleasure of watching you and Dad dancing again. It was a wonderful moment! It made the following things spring to mind:

I love the way you move through a room,
I love the special relationship you have with Dad,
I love how you've fostered my independence and encouraged me without gushing,
I love your sense of humor and your down-to-earth attitude,
I love your common sense,
I love your cooking,
I love the way you never interfere with affairs of my family, even though at times you are concerned,
I love your generosity of spirit,
I love that you're my mom.

All my love,
Sue

Today I watched my brother and his wife, the way they were around each other. I noticed how they sat close together in the restaurant booths, shoulders touching. How when they corrected one another's account of an event, there was no arguing, and generally the corrected one would acquiesce. During the course of the afternoon I was reminded how selfless they are, as they mentioned their volunteer work in the antique orange groves, now on state land designated as a park, how they take the extra oranges to the homeless and work both with their church and the food bank to guarantee that families will not go hungry. How they continue to provide for their son and his family as the young couple works on their advanced degrees. How Gloria nurtures her grandchild, both in body and mind, and the way she interacted with my grandchild during their visit to us up north. Their interest in food and cooking and gardening and home improvement.

Today as my brother drove us to the restaurant and then walked through the parking lot, I was suddenly struck by his profile and his walk and how much they were Dad's. I began thinking of Gloria's giving nature and thought of Mom.

They could certainly do worse, being compared to my folks.

Things get a little sketchy after this. At some point I am taken into emergency to see Jeff, and what I see is shocking. He is unconscious, and there is some sort of tube just off-center on the upper back of his head that appears to be attached directly to his scalp, or beneath it. His hair and head are bloody, and his color is sallow – he looks like someone who has been beaten up. He is limp. The emergency neurologist there has a pained smile on his face as he explains that Jeff has experienced a major brain hemorrhage, and that they are allowing the excess blood to drain out through that hollow bolt. I have never heard of such a device, but I suppose it makes sense. The doctor tells me that they will be watching Jeff during the night and that I can see him for fifteen minutes every two hours once he is moved to intensive care, but to give them some time to settle him in. He also tells me that when the shifts change, there are to be no visitors during that time.

Back out to the waiting room I go, tucking my purse behind my knees to keep it safe. You must understand, this is a county facility in the Inland Empire of Southern California, so all manner of people are there seeking aid. About half of the room is filled with gang members and their families; the poverty all around is fairly evident. There is little to no eye contact between the tight little groups. So I try to protect my belongings and myself as best I can between visits to Jeff, which are brief and only serve to remind me that he is still alive. But I pretend he can hear me and speak low and soothingly, reassuring him that I am there and that he will be OK. Then I go back out to the waiting room, and I wait.

His natural expression isn't smiling. The gray moustache, often irregularly cut, curves around a full-lipped mouth which flat-lines most of the time. I noticed early on that when he was around a female he smiled more freely, and even on the phone his voice would lilt up several tones. It isn't a flirtatious effect but rather a subconscious attempt to appear less threatening. These mannerisms are copied, I found, from his father and are also seen in his younger brother. But around those he lives with he can relax, and the mouth reverts to its default state.

His level of animation and engagement with other members of his conversational circle increase, however, if they are his parents or siblings, or if he started in on a home-brewed glass of Ponderosa Porter or goblet of chianti. Then he becomes a Jeff who can easily participate in the give and take of banter and deeper topics. He might even initiate after a couple of drinks — generally his upward limit. I often wonder what else might help him relax and be more social.

Those times when he can cut loose are invaluable to the rest of us, or at least to me. Those pointy, sparse Spock eyebrows rise, the laughter erupts from deep in his gut, the slouch of his long, thick torso in the dining room chair approaches a forty-five degree angle, one knee crosses over the other, his hands join over his belly and the smile blooms. If the laughter makes his eyes water, off come the coke-bottle-bottom glasses and up comes his t-shirt to clean the heavy lenses of the salty clouds. Waggling his upraised, usually booted foot, Jeff fully connects to the chat, to the moment, to us.

What would make him comfortable the rest of the time? How could he be put at ease? More than thirty years of marriage had certainly removed some of the constraints which bound him to silence much of the time, less likely to start an exchange, although always responsive to another's questions. It gave me pause when Unocal released its scientists, and he started to freelance, becoming a consultant who had to sell his lab safety abilities around the world and then eventually taking a job as a customer service representative for a chemistry lab equipment sales and service company. Suddenly he was thrust into an occupation requiring far more human contact than before. He did well, rose to the occasion, but then I began to think these new situations were contributing to his gradual rise in blood pressure.

So I treasured the times when he visibly relaxed and just talked, and listened. Over the years I learned how to distinguish when would be good times for talks, when to tiptoe, when to focus on housework and shush the kids, how to avoid an outburst (rare, but scary). And yet when I finally revealed those adaptations to him after an argument, he seemed baffled. He had no idea the effect his outward expressions had on others. And how could he know that I was spending my time with him working on what I perceived was a requirement to keep things peaceful around him?

How many of my conclusions about his needs were erroneous? With a taciturn man it's hard to know. I had had three and a half decades to get to know him better; at no point did I ever feel I really did.

Jeffy arrives at the hospital at about six in the morning, and I go home with him to shower, change, and eat. I also sneak over to my computer to let Jadey, with whom I was chatting the night before, know what was going on. I decide to post an announcement on my Star Wars fanfiction website, A-Larger-World, to cover all my online buddies.

Dear Friends,

Last evening at about 6 p.m., my beautiful, intelligent husband Jeff suffered a stroke here at our home. He is currently in intensive care, having been airlifted to a hospital about a half-hour from our home. He will be undergoing some procedures over the next few days to determine his prognosis. I remained with him at the hospital during the night, since I was allowed to spend fifteen minutes with him every two hours, and will stay with him as long as it helps.

I will be here at home only for a few minutes a day to shower and change and grab some coffee. If you want, I'll keep you posted on his recovery.

If you are a person who believes in the power of prayer, please offer some up for Jeff. He has always been an active, brilliant man and a wonderful, understanding and supportive husband, father and grandfather. His family needs him. I need him.

Please, those of you who have been the movers and shakers here (you know who you are), keep things going. Don't let this amazing community fall apart. I want to see you all here, writing, nurturing one another's efforts and growing as authors and artists when I am able to get back.

Keep the vision alive, please.

Sue

I am a product of small houses that required closed doors for away time
Hours spent alone on my bed or staring out the window at worlds found in
Superhero comic books, science fiction novels
Listening to familiar songs hummed, whistled and sung a capella
While family tended lush lawns and luxurious landscape
Smelling wonderful things being baked down the hall
Hearing laughter that tugged at my lips
TV during and after dinner dictating mealtime conversation
Stretching and contracting metal hallway heater - a monster's gait in the night
Warm dog curled at my belly
As I dream of an alternate universe

During the ensuing days I check in on my site and livejournal blog when I can. The support which is offered is heartwarming, to say the least. But I have no time to do any other online investigations of the kind of stroke Jeff had suffered. Perhaps I subconsciously put on blinders so as to just deal with the evidence before my eyes.

I should have known...

When my sister-in-law, Donna, heard the diagnosis, she immediately looked it up on the internet. I didn't have the luxury of time at that point, those awful ten days, nor the knowledge. Being the constant optimist, I overlooked the kindly smiles of the medical staff, interpreting them as a nice bedside manner. After all, Jeff had waved at me when I came into his room the next day! Stymied by the breathing tubes and stuck in ICU psychosis, he was unable to be consulted on the issue of his sudden, massive brain hemorrhage, nor the potential outcomes. The near inevitability of the prognosis was lost on us both, and the neurologists at that first hospital weren't exactly fountains of information.

But, really? I should have known. It would be a rare occurrence to survive a brain bleed of that magnitude and much less likely to emerge from it intact. I mean, he was posturing before they even loaded him into the ambulance to take him across the street to the park for the airlift.

But, man, the relief, when he waved at me the next day! Hearing him talk when the tubes came out — he's still in there, all there! At USC days later when the dominoes of secondary strokes began to hit, and he lost strength and movement on his right side, I was still upbeat, encouraging him to work on his breathing treatments and use his left hand to feed himself.

No problem. I'll go on sabbatical from teaching, we'll have a new diet plan, throw out all the beer and wine you've brewed, and take long walks together. We can beat this. Things don't happen to us. This is the kind of stuff that rips apart the lives of others, but not us...

Well, I know it now. Sometimes things like this can happen to even us.

Shifting my attention to work, I find the home phone number of my principal and call him. Realizing that it's Sunday, and that he treasures his family time, I try to keep it short. When I tell him that my husband has had a stroke, his nearly involuntary response is "Oh, no." I am sure in his mind he is connecting the dots just as I have – this is a high-maintenance class, even though it is just first grade.

"You need to call Michelle Luparello. She has worked with the kids before and can handle whatever comes up. There won't be any sub plans. She will have to rely on my first grade team. Renee Norton can give her what she needs to get through the first day." I am thankful that Renee teaches right next door to me and that we have a bi-fold door pass-through that will ensure that Michelle is not so isolated. Mentally, I note that I need to get all of the paperwork I had taken home over to Robin so she can deliver it to my classroom. Right away Gary reassures me that the staff will take care of everything.

At some schools the staff maintains a very cubicle attitude, teaching in a bubble. Part of the reason for the massive success Marshall School has achieved is that they don't subscribe to that methodology. Especially with my first grade team, for years we have acted as if we were all in this together, both within and across grade levels. At a time like this, everyone will pull together to make sure that Michelle gets all the support she needs. And just like that – I dismiss it. I no longer have to be concerned about my students or my job.

The Second Night

The next night, I was able to post this on my website, after reading many messages of prayer and good wishes:

You guys are all so wonderful…

Last night at around 4:00 a.m., Jeff waved to me when he caught sight of me in the room! I was on the opposite side of the bed and took his hand, and he squeezed it tightly! Then, a few minutes later, he moved his legs, stretching them. He hadn't done that before! The LVN came in and asked him to wiggle his toes, and he could!

So I got to stay in his room til 6! YAY! No lobby full of gangbangers and babymamas!! I mean it, you guys, this was NOT a place to be alone. So I tried to be unobtrusive. I think I blew that today, though. I kept hauling the nurses and respirator folks back into the room to fix things and make him comfortable.

I am going to try to stay home and sleep tonight. Jeff got off the ventilator this evening after coming off the drugs for the angiogram. He can TALK! He can fully participate in conversations! He has a big headache and so they put him on lotsa drugs. Blood pressure still has to be totally drugged out to cooperate. And I think if I am not in there jumping up every time something beeps or the numbers on the monitors don't look right to me, he might sleep a little better, too.

ALTHOUGH, he sure seems to like it when I sit in the chair next to him, snake my hand through the slats and hold his hand…

Yesterday at about 6:10 p.m. my husband had come downstairs to tell me he thought he needed help. Perhaps ten minutes later, he had passed out. Last night, at 7:30 p.m., my husband was in deep coma, posturing, groaning animalistically, combative, and very near death. They put a bolt in his head to drain off the liquid that was pressing on his brain and spinal column (which has so far amounted to a third of a liter!), and within a few hours I had my husband back.

Wrote this sitting next to him early today (grabbed my journal on the way out the door after showering and changing):

Blinding pain
explosion
nausea
darkness

Suspended twilight time
muffled sounds, regular, alien rhythm
the unfamiliar confounds

Voiceless frustration
helpless husk
gestures and nods can't convey the soul
stroked by God

The Hand of the Creator
humbles and silences
but cannot, will not
extinguish this creative mind

I sit and await
the reawakening

He has a long way to go before he can come home. The cause of the break needs
to be fully determined. The blood pressure must be controlled. It has been
discovered he is developing diabetes. Lots of lifestyle changes are going to be
needed here, for all of us, if it's going to work: our view of what our job responsibilities are (I called both our bosses this morning and told them we wouldn't
be back for a LONG TIME), incorporating regular exercise in our routines, getting back to basic cooking that is low-fat and containing lots of vegetables, and
the whole sugar angle, including the beer and wine Jeff loves to brew and we
both enjoy drinking. That one is flat out gonna have to go.

But, dammit. . .

I wrote this as I sat next to his later bed today. . .

THIS CHANGES EVERYTHING

Perspective, prospects,
lives ruled by ferocious work ethic
are halted irrefutably
by words on a chart:
HYPERTENSION,

STROKE,
DIABETES.

Our lifestyles flirted with deadly outcomes.
Vocations dictate fatal behaviors,
only if we refuse to change.

I am in this relationship for the long haul:
richer/poorer
better/worse
sickness/health

All the right choices that eluded us before
are now laid at our feet.
We will be richer if we have one another.

We shall embrace this offering of
A SECOND CHANCE
for 33 more years of love
and life
together.

A huge thank you to everyone who held good thoughts for us here. Magic works.

Even with the mess at the top of his head, Jeff looks resplendent to me. I can't get over that he has lived through this, and with all cognitive functions intact. I can see in his eyes that he is all there. I ask him if he wants his glasses on, because he is close to blind without them. I know firsthand how frustrating it is to be unable to see across a room, and it certainly would be worse in an unfamiliar place. So I take the heavy glasses off the counter and place them on his face, over those beautiful light green eyes.

At first glance, he appeared to be similar to the other students milling about in the hallway. The classroom we huddled around hadn't emptied out yet, so we awkwardly lined the walls, trying to stay out of the way of those working their way to the stairwell or elevator. No eye contact. Each of us a stranger to the rest, attending just another general ed. class at Cal State Fullerton.

But I glanced over at him when he wasn't looking. At least, I assumed from the angle of his head that he was peering at something else besides me. With those very dark sunglasses, it was impossible to tell.

They were thick, those shades — clearly corrective lenses leading the nearly blind. The frames were faded black and just as thick. Earpieces slid back into a mop of long chestnut brown hair that skirted and curled around his collar. It seemed that he had spent little time trying to manage that substantial amount of hair, and the cut was far from perfect.

He wasn't very tall, but, then, I have always found tall guys intimidating. However, his muscles pushing their way around under the short-sleeved shirt revealed a young man to be reckoned with. Long torso, short legs, interesting turquoise and silver belt buckle. I caught what details I could between glances.

The class finally spilled out of the room and we, the waiters, swiveled to enter. My eyes drifted back to him just before we walked in, and I could tell this time that he was looking at me behind those shades because he gave me a little smile and graciously held the door for me.

The Downfall of Love

interrupting my education
with your silence behind dense glasses
thick, soft lips asking to be met
no phd when your child sprouts within me

living in the hotbed of the inland empire
rasping through smog and car exhaust from the neighborly freeway
cranking out kids and jars of jam
fighting the never-ending battle of dust
instead of reams of translations

altering my future with your middle-class expectations
and tight hugs
pulling my fingers through your untamed chestnut, then silver strands
my hands meet around your middle, cheek on grease-stained shirt
while others gather data from the field and natives call them "doctor"

my people call me "Mrs. Parsons" in the classroom, Mom in the kitchen,
grandma on the beach
and honey in bed
all would have been unknown to me, and so many would not have known life
but for the downfall of love

it's all your fault
you are to blame
mysterious boy with dark sunglasses and quiet demeanor
inviting me into your life
your arms
your heart

He didn't say much and didn't volunteer in class (which I did enough to make up for both of us). And with my lack of experience, I didn't know what to say to catch his attention. Luckily, there was a chance he was interested, too, since he followed a group of us down to the student union after class one day. A bunch of us had a break before the next class and had decided to grab a snack.

This became our routine. I worked to fit into this new group, but wound up alienating myself when one of the boys made what I considered to be a racist statement — I can't even recall now what it was — and in my outrage I shamed him before his peers. Leaving the table, I found I was somewhat shocked at what I had done.

The next day that we had Spanish class, Jeff followed a couple of us who remained in the reformed group down to the Union. I was awfully glad he hadn't chosen to stay with the preppie group.

To this day, I am unsure how long this arrangement lasted, but, for me, it seemed to go on forever with no change. I certainly enjoyed being with Jeff in the group, but wondered how to let him know I was wanting more. One evening, in frustration, I wrote out a poem about him on the back of a notebook that I was sure he would never see, saying things that I needed to get out of my system. The only line I can recall was the first — "Jeff, please hurry…" This teenager was still too tongue-tied to say any of that stuff to his face.

Days later, we were back in the basement of the science building and I decided to grab a yogurt from the concession area. Apparently, as I stood in line, Jeff had started messing with my stack of books, flipping them over. He caught sight of the offending poem and quickly read it. By the time I got back to the table, everything was back in its place. It was months before Jeff revealed to me what he had done, but, clearly, something had changed.

As we headed up the stairs after our break, I turned to see if he was still following me. He was conversing with a buddy of ours a couple of stairs behind. Without stopping or looking up, he reached up and touched the small of my back to encourage me to keep climbing, that they were right there. The electricity of that first touch, even through my clothes, makes me smile and tingle in response even to this day.

The proverbial ice was broken. Shortly after that, we had our first "date". Broke students, all we could afford at that point was to go to one another's house or meet on campus. He came over, met my parents, and Jeff and I made candles, melting the wax on the stovetop and adding scent and color. I had bought some metal forms for us to shape the tapers. Afterwards I walked him out, but he didn't leave for some time as we kissed, Jeff leaning on the garage door and pulling me close.

A few evenings later, on my drive home from work at the Huntington Beach Public

Library, I sat at the stoplight at Main St. and Beach Blvd. in stunned, gleeful disbelief. I was in love! I had actually fallen in love with a guy! All those years — well, three of them — that I had checked out boys, very briefly dated three of them, I had always felt somewhat strange when they moved to hold my hand or kiss me. Honestly, it had felt all wrong. It got to the point where I wondered if it would ever feel RIGHT.

A movie with friends, perhaps a quick dinner somewhere cheap, and more time with a group of girls I eventually moved in with a few months later…things developed quickly. He got the keys to his dad's sailboat out near Long Beach Marina and we did some what they used to call "heavy petting". Man, I never pet my dog that way! But I also had never been turned on by a guy like this. Despite my Catholic upbringing, I had glommed onto what my parents had been displaying in front of God and mankind every day of their marriage — they were in love and lusted after one another. They showed their affection in non-offensive ways every time they were in a room together. I decided almost without conscious thought that I was going to make love with this boy and had absolutely no regrets about it. He would be my first and my last.

By the next week Jeff and I were having The Conversation™ in his car. He declared that if I were to get pregnant it would just solidify the relationship more. We would get married. He said he felt married already. If I had had any doubts prior to that moment, they melted away. This was the man I was going to spend the rest of my life with.

Looking at my internal calendar, I could see that my period was about to begin, so that following weekend would be our first tryst. With boat keys, a blanket, a bottle of sauvignon blanc and a tray of pastries for dinner since we had no appetite for food, and with no contraception we set off. For hours we experimented with lovemaking awkwardly but with lots of affection on a tiny single-wide berth in his dad's sailboat. Eventually the space heater and light blew a fuse on the dock, and it was time to go. My makeup was a horrendous mess, I discovered as we hit a Denny's nearby (open all night). We had rung in the New Year, big time.

I can't recall now how late I got in. It was a blessed relief, though, that I had excommunicated myself, because that allowed me not only to sleep in, but also to avoid familial contact 'til about noon when my parents and Nanny got back from church.

I wasn't a coffee drinker at that point, being barely out of my teens, but I set up the old tin percolator anyway. It might have been a reason for me to have my late night overlooked when the rest of my family arrived, ready for breakfast.

Man, my hips ached. Every muscle in my lower torso protesting walking, sitting, being. Part strain, part cramps, thank God. Taking a minute away from the cereal, the aromatic brew and the L.A. Times comics, I blew out a little prayer of gratefulness for a New Year, the gift of the worse period I had ever had and the lovely young man who had caused it all.

Soon after, I told my mom what Jeff and I were up to. My mother and I had shared nearly everything. I had a pretty open relationship with my parents — not that I ever had had much to tell. I remember my mom standing in the doorway as I prepared to go to bed one night, and I told her that I was so happy, and I loved Jeff so much, I wanted to share my happiness with her. Unfortunately, this news did not make HER happy at all. She told me it would have been better had I not said anything about it at all, that good Catholic girls waited for marriage, like she had. My attempt to fill her in about how things had changed fell on deaf ears.

The next day my father, however, had a different viewpoint. He clapped me on the shoulder and laughed softly as he rejoiced, "I was beginning to think you were a lesbian!" (Keep in mind that this was 1971.) Hmmm…while it was true that I was not the most feminine gal on the planet, I had always indicated an interest in boys. It must have been my lack of dating that concerned him. Well, no more worries on that score now!

Soon after that, I made plans to move out of my home. I had two friends, Debbie and Carolyn, who were also ready to release those apron strings. We found an absolutely horrible old decrepit house in Anaheim on a corner, across from the high school. Later we discovered it had been condemned, but the owner had made just enough improvements to keep it rentable. A two-story craftsman-style, it was dark and foreboding dried-out cedar shake on the outside, much like the stereotypical haunted house in an older neighborhood. Inside, the rooms were lovely, with a great deal of woodwork that would look beautiful if refinished, a fireplace that might work someday, two bedrooms upstairs and one down. Since Carolyn had some ambulation issues, she took the downstairs bedroom, and Debbie and I the ones upstairs. The kitchen was not remodeled and had no appliances. We would be unable to cook and had no fridge to store food. The place was crawling with ants wherever the tiniest morsel of food was left out. I tried living on peanut butter on toast for the six weeks we lived there, and became ill whenever I tried to eat. We got a kitten who took care of the cockroach problem.

It was clear that this place was not going to work out. We abandoned our plans to paint and sand and moved to a triplex in Garden Grove — much newer and cleaner, no pests, and with a heater! It was only two bedrooms, so Carolyn shared with a different friend, Sue, and I got a bedroom to myself again.

All this moving out and having my own bedroom stuff made it awfully nice for Jeff and me. No more boat with fuse-blowing heaters freezing us out of our bunk! Still a narrow twin bed, the one I had brought from my parents' home, but all ours. Now we had a kitchen in which we could practice cooking food for a better-rounded diet. We took turns with chores, had a laundry room below our unit, and could bring alcohol in with abandon — well, whenever we could afford to, which was rare.

On occasion we would meet back at Debbie's. She had been unable to afford to stay out on her own and had moved back into her parents' apartment in Buena Park. Perhaps six times while still in college, one of us would provide a baggie of marijuana and share the delight with the others. Sue and Carolyn weren't interested in this, so Jeff and I and Debbie and, occasionally, her sister would have a spaced-out evening with music — often Joni Mitchell, the Byrds, or Judy Collins.

Jeff couldn't get into grass. He found that he would hallucinate with it — not unpleasantly — but didn't like the lack of control it imparted. And at fifteen dollars a baggie, it wasn't the cheapest form of entertainment, even shared with others. A bottle of Spanada or Boone's Farm Strawberry Hill had a similar effect and cost perhaps a dollar fifty a bottle. Plus, those were legal. Jeff was over 21 and could buy it at the store. I was underage, still, but the problems created with allowing me to drink were far less troublesome that having everyone smoke an illegal substance. I recall a time it was my turn to supply the stuff. A boy where I worked, the Huntington Beach Public Library, was stoned just about every day, and he sold me a baggie at work. I was absolutely petrified as I hid it in the glove compartment of my car and drove more carefully than I ever had in my life up to Deb's parents' apartment. I felt extremely fortunate not to be the supplier after that.

In the fall of 1971 I took my last B.A. class in Linguistics by mail, because the professor for it was spending the year in Spain. He would mail me assignments which I would complete and send back to him then wait for the next packet to arrive. That winter, Sue and Carolyn decided they would move to a different place in the spring, one they liked better, in a nicer neighborhood. Jeff and I had decided to get married that September, so instead of moving to place on my own, and unable to talk Jeff into moving out with me, I relocated back at my folks' house. Working full-time, I tried to save up some money for when Jeff and I could be together.

Our lovely days and nights of having a room to ourselves were temporarily over. And the boat keys had been inexplicably moved from their normal location on the pegboard near the kitchen door at Jean and Howard's house. We both had classes during the day when my parents worked, and my schedule at the library ate up a lot of other hours. There really was no time for us to be alone at my house or Jeff's, whose grandmother lived at his house full-time.

These were desperate times for the young lovers. One night we smooched in his dad's truck parked in front of my house until four in the morning. So, these also became frustrating times, going from 60 to zero overnight.

At this point, my birth control pills ran out, so off to the clinic I went for a refill. A group of us girls sat in the waiting room for quite some time, with no one being called in to see the doctor or nurse. Finally, a receptionist came out and informed us that the doctor had been called off on an emergency and would not be coming in that day. As we all filed out, I realized that I had cut this office visit too close. By the time there was another appointment, it would be too late for me to begin a new set of pills. I would have to wait a month before my cycle came around to another start time. And that meant a month of...no nookie.

Had that been the case, this story would have had a far different ending.

Two weeks into our abstinence, Jeff and I were on the couch at my parents' house, and my parents were asleep down the hall. We had a lovely time. After, Jeff looked into my eyes, squinting because his glasses were on the coffee table, and asked, a bit breathlessly, if we were OK. After a moment, I intoned, "Nooooooo......" I was kinda surprised he had asked. I knew he could count as well as I could. Counting...check. Head on straight? Not so much. Ruled by hormones? You bet!

So, a couple of weeks later, my period hadn't started. And it didn't, for many, many months after that.

A trip to the doctor confirmed what I had feared. Yes, I was pregnant. Very much so. The theory was, if you just come off birth control pills, you are likely to be more fertile, especially two weeks in during your normal ovulation time. My eggs apparently had been rarin' to go, after so many months of having been denied access to that lovely uterine wall.

I called Jeff to let him know and to ask him to tell his parents, as I would tell mine. And I called to set a date at the county courthouse for us to get married, as we had agreed.

My future mother-in-law had agreed for us to have a little family reception at her house, and to make my dress. We picked out a lovely pattern for a long, angel-sleeved dress and some muted yellow floral material with a bit of lace. She began to make the dress and was nearly finished, seeming very excited about the preparations. I was grateful that Jean was happy to have me as a daughter-in-law and that she was so warm and welcoming as I approached the day when I would become part of her family. And she didn't appear to be fazed as to the rush job — she was getting only two weeks to pull all this together. Finally, one day I asked her about that. And I discovered Jeff hadn't told her she was about to become a grandmother. Nor had he told his dad. It was clear that he considered himself irresponsible to have "knocked me up", and, at nearly 26, he should have known better.

Since I had spilled the beans to his mother, I insisted he tell his dad. Well, he didn't. Jean did. But both of them seemed delighted, in any case. And my parents really liked Jeff, so things appeared to be working out fine.

I felt lousy, of course. It was summer, it was hot, and I was fairly miserable. As we stood in front of the county judge and I wished someone had recorded the words he was saying, I *realized that life was suddenly moving very fast. I was 21 years old, I had a bachelor's degree, had moved out of my parents' home, fallen in love, was pregnant and was getting married.*

My brother and his fiancée stood up for us, which was fitting, since they were getting married the following month (empty-nesting the heck out of my parents!). During the reception, I fled out to the water feature in Jean and Howard's backyard to cool off. Jean had arranged for a friend of hers to make a small, but very nice wedding cake, my mom and aunt had brought some of their yummy standard favorites, and I think there were cold cuts. I honestly don't remember.

I do recall getting a gigantically tall bottle of Galliano, the banana-flavored liqueur one uses to make Harvey Wallbangers, and a set of corning ware from my grandparents.

I am given the clothes he had been wearing when the paramedics took him off to the medical center. It is clear that they were rapidly torn off him when he got to the hospital, so I am not sure why they saved them for me, but here they are in a bag. I go ahead and take them home, putting them on the floor of the bedroom near his closet door after I go home that night. For now, I am unsure whether to keep them or not. They hold his scent, but it is tinged with something foreign to me. Fear?

Jeff never was much of one for appearance. Wardrobe-wise, you could clone his father's closet and dresser drawers, multiply it by two, and you would have what he, Jeff and Jeff's brother, Brad, wore. All you would need to do would be to occasionally change logos; Brad would be your smaller size, Jeff in the middle and Howard the husky. But the actual items of clothing would pretty much be the same.

Let's begin with shoes. The guys all had the same gait, rolling out with toes turned out, so the wear on the shoes would be identical. Florsheim's for the workday, lace-up and brown or black, and multi-holed sneakers with paint and grass stains for the weekend. But no shoes around the house, usually. One or two pairs of work shoes, maybe two pairs of sneakers. The latter used to be white.

Jeff liked his slippers. On a trip up to see Shauna in the Great Northwest, he discovered shearling-lined suede bootie slippers at Costco. Shauna had wanted a pair for Christmas, and Jeff fell in love with them as well. Great for wearing around the house in the winter, even in Chino, Inland Valley, Southern California.

Socks? Holy. Or Holey? With holes. When you marry a woman who doesn't darn socks, you get holey ones. They come in a six-pack with no holes, originally, and are cheap cotton ones for the weekends, under those yucky sneakers. They might be tube socks. Black orlon blend, which pill mercilessly, for the workdays.

Moving up, we have pants. There are two kinds: one for work, one for work at home. There is no actual "play". Levi's Action Slacks, with a scosh more room, works for all three guys. Or maybe even J. C. Penney's version thereof. Nicer Dockers, perhaps. In any case, navy blue, black, dark brown, khaki. That way, they will go with all, and I mean ALL, of the shirts we will discuss shortly. Women would never combine colors the way these guys do.

Now, weekends, it's jeans. Levi's 501 for the younger guys, older action slacks for Howard. All of them look as though they have been the weekend pants choice for several years. All of them have holes in various interesting places, ripped up bottom hems due to the short legs the guys were afflicted with and the fact that jeans generally don't come that short for older gentlemen. Paint and wood stain splotches required. Engine grease is good, too. Perhaps some acid fades for additional flavor.

In all cases, most of the jeans should be too small, built for a time when the man's weight was several pounds less. This causes a bit of belly rollover, but it's all good. There's more solidarity for the Parsons males that way.

Now we advance upward to the shirts. For the working gentleman, we have solids or stripes, and the occasional pale, light-colored plaid or geometric pattern. There will be no cranberry or puce for Jeff or Howard, but there may be a little of that for the more adventuresome Bradley. The older two guys wear white, perhaps a pale yellow or green, very light blue. For dress-up, our daughter Jeremie recalls a pseudo-Western shirt they all had, worn, of course, with cowboy boots. They had no cowboy hats unless you count the ten gallon white plastic hardhats Howard and Jean bought them all one Christmas. Shirts will be worn until they can be seen through, as they fade and develop fraying hems and paper-thin elbow areas. Jeff's employer, Thermo-Electron, provided logo polo shirts, navy blue or black, for their customer service engineers, which made it convenient and thrifty for those involved.

The weekend? Anything goes with shirts. Mainly, it's tees with beer or wine sayings such as "Life is a Cabernet", "Wineaux", or the one Shauna designed for the whole family — "Parsons Wine — when quantity, versus quality, is your criteria for a good wine". The same types of stains found on the weekend pants also apply here. Older shirts formerly worn to work are fine, until your wife decides to start tearing them off your body one sleeve or pocket at a time. (Jean, my mother-in-law, taught me how to do this. It's hilarious. You grab hold of a piece of the offending garment, currently being worn by the hapless victim, and call out, "Oh! Oh, dear! What's happening here?!?!?" as you slowly tear along a seam which no longer holds much together due to the thread having become rotten. Once you have a section off, you find another weak point and start again. The wearer is not visibly amused during this process.) T-shirts also provide a fun alternative to this game, since they tear in the middle of the larger segments quite nicely. They also have a tendency to shrink in unappealing ways, exposing bellies protruding from tight jeans.

If it gets cold on a Saturday or Sunday, count on an old jacket coming out of the closet, preferably one that blends in with the stain types found on the other clothing du jour. One of Jeff's favorites was the one he got from Bastanchury Water Company. Once it got too small for him his son took it over and wears it to this day. It's amazing it has held together this long. Brad and Howard might be more likely to wear fleece, but Jeff's preference was generally cloth. Once he was exposed to Woolies and Pete's, wool and alpaca sweater companies, he began to purchase and wear that type around the house on frigid evenings and always wore them when we traveled up to Bellingham in the winter. However, these extra nice pieces never made an appearance in the garage.

Another older outwear piece Jeff favored was a plaid flannel-type overshirt with the most garish colors, featuring turquoise, imaginable. Unfortunately, his son also retrieved that when I thought I had discarded it and continues to wear it to assault my eyes whenever possible.

Watch caps were preferred by all three men for winter warmth. Jeff, especially, needed something warm around his face due to his "cold-nose syndrome". When he was in eighth grade, he suffered from repeated nosebleeds and resultant blood loss over a few weeks' time. The doctor had no choice but to cauterize the bleeders, which caused Jeff to have reduced blood flow to his nose. With lowered circulation, that meant less warm blood heating up the area, thus the cold nose. It was rather shocking in the winter to kiss his warm mouth and come into contact with a frosty nasal appendage. Of course, he always thought my reaction was comical.

Now we come to the out-there jackets and coats. Jeff did have a lovely London Fog trench coat for traveling or for the unusual cold and rainy days where we lived. We had found it at an outlet mall north of where our oldest, Shauna, lived in Bellingham, up by the Canadian border. I doubt we could have found one so easily or for so low a price in Southern California.

However, it was natural for him to combine his love of jackets – he was a total jacket whore (I should talk. My sweater and jacket collections are unparalleled) – with his enjoyment at the sewing machine. Jeff had discovered Frostline, a company which offered kits from which one could make outdoor gear such as tents, sleeping bags, parkas, even backpacks, many of the garments with down insulation. He had a lovely time sealing the nylon ripstop material with a soldering iron, and then the feathers would fly as he stuffed the baffles he had sewn with goose down. Consequently, Jeff developed a wonderful collection of parkas with varying levels of insulation. One rusty orange jacket he made for me was incredibly warm, which I welcomed, but not so much the Michelin Man effect the baffles gave me. Eventually, of course, his expertise qualified him to create his own designs. His clothing, tents, stuff sacks and backpacks have stood the test of time, with very few leaks (of feathers) and no tears. With the amount of hiking and camping with Boy Scouts, that is quite a track record. As I recall, one of his heavy down jackets has some campfire ash stains on it, but guys usually consider that a badge of honor.

Brad caught on to the camping gear construction and has a similar collection of parkas and sleeping bags, but Howard never quite got into the sewing. Besides, Jean felt she was the owner of their sewing machine and didn't give up that power without a fight. Also, her trepidation about how the machine might be returned to her, if at all, was a valid concern.

At night, Jeff wore pajamas – flannel in the winter and broadcloth the rest of the year. He wore them until the holes prevented their staying on his body. However, he had a wonderful wool bathrobe which resembled a flannel-type pattern, bluish green plaid over navy blue, that he took good care of, always hanging it on a hook in the closet between wearings. It had a tie sash for closure. I must say, he looked quite dapper in that robe. Also, it covered up the tattered jammies he had on underneath.

Sizewise, Jeff went from a size medium when we married to a large thirty years later, which could have been predicted from looking at this father, who had done the same gain decades before. However, he remained just as strong and muscular due to his constant puttering around the house and the outdoor activities he did with the Boy Scouts and his brother. Only in his late 50s did I begin to hear some wheezing during more demanding activities. Also, his back had begun to give him a lot of trouble, not only with his work around the house on the weekends, but also his sedentary job hours. Much of his time was spent at the business desk at home doing paperwork and making calls, and then sitting in traffic when he was assigned to a lab in the Los Angeles area for a day. And the slouch he generally assumed when seated mimicked his father's. All of the Parsons guys had long torsos and short legs — Corgi-style — so their spines took the brunt of any torqueing activity, lifting and twisting. In his mid-to-late fifties Jeff was beginning to show that discomfort by leaning slightly forward and bowing his knees outward as he walked, stiffly.

His age showed in his hair as well. When I met him, Jeff had a shock of very thick, long brown hair that reached past his collar and brushed his shoulders. His mom would cut it for him from time to time in their backyard, and she used thinning shears to try to make it lay a bit flatter. Still, it would wave and curl a bit at the ends, and he would rake his fingers through it to keep it from flopping in his face. By the time he hit his 40s it was thinning itself, and had begun to gray. The graying happened quickly, over the space of perhaps four years, and by the time he was in his late 40s it was a beautiful silver, not unlike his father's. A bit of receding had begun as well, and he had a bit of a widow's peak in the center of his forehead. The bright gray hair brought out his light green eyes even more than the brown had, but, unfortunately, he had to go back to wearing those coke-bottle-bottom glasses when the contact lenses bothered him too much. He couldn't really wear the contacts in the lab, anyway; he would have had to wear safety goggles over them, which would defeat the whole purpose of wearing contacts.

Hair had begun to grow in other interesting places, as well. I noticed the nose and ear hair begin to get out of control right about the time the massive graying had set in. And the edges of his moustache would curve up in random arcs, along with some of his eyebrow hair. All in all, he began to resemble a mad scientist, from time to time. He would maximize that look with a maniacal expression — eyebrows hitting the ceiling, eyes bugging out and mouth agape — just for dramatic effect. Each of his children mimicked this total look at Halloween on various years, adding his old acid-stained lab jacket to complete the package.

If I have overstated or caricatured Jeff's appearance, then let me temper it this way: I rarely felt prouder than when Jeff would walk into my school office to talk with me after school, or when we went out somewhere together. I was terribly pleased to be his wife, and to be seen with him. I felt he was handsome, if not debonair or romantic; he had fathered intelligent and attractive children, had been an excellent provider and helpmate, had been everything one would need a husband to be. He was interesting, well-read, and came from a wonderful family. So the quirks and chinks in his armor, to me, made him all the more endearing. Bring on the ear hair. This silver fox is mine.

The Third Night

I spend the day at the hospital, then return late that evening to post this on my livejournal account:

OK, so now I see that this is a cruise, and every day we sail into a new, uncharted port. Upon disembarking, Jeff and I discover that we have no knowledge of the culture or language at this new place, and we have to learn it as we go along.

Today was about patience and repetition, and I discovered just how much faith we have in each other.

Jeff had no recollection of the past two days. That is certainly a merciful thing; however it also meant he had no clue where he was or why he was here. So his mind made things up for him as he went along.

By the time I got there this morning he had already concluded, at first, that he was in the Philippines (the first nurse who visited him was from there, and Jeff HAD worked there for several weeks), then Texas, and finally we were in Phoenix. We remained in Phoenix for most of the day, until we finally landed in San Diego. At times we were in a hotel room for a business convention, and it was nice that I was visiting him, but shouldn't I go check in? Climb on in here with me... hmmm... this bed would have been too small for us even right after we got married, when we were both thinner... At other times, most of the time, in fact, we were in a lab somewhere, surrounded by gas chromatographs and mass spectrometers, and he occasionally was fishing around in the bed for a remote to watch a TV that wasn't there. The incredibly heavy devotion to the job was clearly evident to me. He was fixated. No wonder...

So my job was this: every ten to fifteen minutes, I became a recording, reminding him of where we were, why we were there. Every ten to fifteen minutes I had to jump up and put my hand on his chest to keep him from trying to get out of bed (he couldn't figure out why he couldn't). Every so often I had to prevent him from ripping out IVs or pulling on the bolt at the top of his head, the one with the drain. That was my job today.

I don't know if it'll be rinse and repeat tomorrow or not. Ship's at sea right now. Hafta learn a new language and culture tomorrow, maybe.

And I'm figuring out more than that. I am finding out what love is all about. He had to accept on his faith in me that I wouldn't lie to him, that my description of reality had more validity than his. And he did that over and over again, despite not remembering anything about the last two days, nor even about what happened half an hour earlier.

We are gonna get through this, and we will be the better for it.

When I first arrive at Jeff's hospital room, he is immersed in a fantasy; not having been prepared for this, I participate in his event, whatever that happens to be. I'm so grateful that he no longer has to be on a respirator, and it is so wonderful to hear his voice, I just play along with whatever he is saying. When a nurse finally passes by, I grab him and ask if Jeff's behavior is normal. The nice young man fills me in; yes, often ICU patients are possessed by what is described as ICU psychosis, where their minds are unable to fully grasp their surroundings and situation, so they invent a situation which is more familiar and comfortable. I can certainly agree that this is a far better scenario than hysterical fear. However, the nurse explains that I can gently reengage Jeff's mind by calmly stating in simple terms what has happened and why he is here.

What I write on my journal page reflects my amazement at how Jeff is able to accept my version of reality because it makes far more sense than his. After all, if he were on a job in a chem. lab somewhere, or traveling abroad for business, why would I be there? He seems rather quizzical about my presence, but his mind just tries to figure out a way to work it all in. The scientist in him needs order and logic. When I supply him with a better conclusion than the one he had worked out, he instantly adopts it.

But there is a point in our conversation when it loops over onto itself. The original scene he was living in fades back into view for him, and his words begin to repeat, the same questions resurface. I realize that he has lost a segment of our visit, and that we are being bumped back into a hotel room or lab. We start over with his illusion, my gentle explanation, his dawning understanding, fade back.

I write this entry in my journal:

Rinse and Repeat

"The Square Dancers
 have checked in
 and so have the administrators
 so we'll need
 to get messages
 from the front desk"

"How was the drive here? It's about as far as Flagstaff, but not as pretty".

"Well, that was easy
 just changed the injector
 on that autosampler...
 Let's check these"

"Well, climb on in...hmmm
 Maybe this bed isn't big enough – not even a double.
 We aren't as small as we used to be"

Honey, you're in a hospital bed. You had a stroke two days ago. Please don't try to get up – you'll detach the monitor feeds. And then they'll have to restrain you.

Second verse, same as the first. Repeat every ten to fifteen minutes ALL DAY LONG.

Because of the psychotic episodes, the nurses do wind up having to restrain Jeff by tying his wrists to the bedframe – otherwise, he begins pulling out IVs, sending the nurses running when the alarms sound. I am frightened at the prospect of his pulling at the bolt on his head. When I mention the stroke and the presence of the bolt, he begins to reach up to examine it, and I have to stop him. My amazement at my patience is only a fraction of the amount of humility I feel that he believes me every time.

For the first few months of our marriage Jeff worked with his father, trying to get a business started. They purchased some scientific instruments and telescope equipment, intending to sell do-it-yourself lens grinding kits, and I was to type up the manual on an electric type-writer Howard provided for me. I had never worked on that style of machine before — one on which different characters had different values based on width — so creating this booklet was very slow going. I did what I could with it evenings, since I still commuted down to the Huntington Beach Public Library for my audio-visual page job during the day.

I was also pregnant with Shauna, due in February, and planned to quit the library job a few weeks before I delivered. We paid off my Datsun in preparation for having little in the way of cash flow until Jeff and Howard's small business took off.

It never did. Luckily, Jeff was able to get a job as plant manager, or so he thought, at Bas-tanchury Water Company — a bottled water plant. This was back in the days when bottled water meant the five-gallon variety of bottle that you would struggle to upend on a cooler.

Once Shauna was born and began to click off milestone after milestone, often a bit early, the mundane routine I established in our little rental house-behind-a-house in Anaheim began to wear on me. She was a busy person, impatient to grow up. I believe from the outset she considered herself a miniature adult. As a result, we began to butt heads. And I needed more adult interaction than was available to me. We had the Datsun, but I really felt I had nowhere to go. Just about everyone I knew worked during the day or was attend-ing school, or both. Cabin fever set in and raged.

When Shauna turned around ten months I started back to school at Cal State Fullerton for my master's degree in Linguistics, attending two classes per semester. Jeff's little road-ster wasn't functional enough at that point, needing a rebuild, so he would often take the Datsun to work. Jean came over on my school days, one day per week and freed me up so I could pack my dinner, walk to the bus stop and head up to the college. At ten, when my second class was over, Jeff would bundle Shauna up and they would come pick me up.

But Jeff's job was trouble. The company was owned by someone who had other interests and would drop by occasionally to ensure that things were being done his way. When he finally discovered that Jeff had been put in charge of the plant, he insisted that Jeff was far too young to take on a job with that level of responsibility. I found all this out when Jeff's TR came flying up onto the front lawn of the duplex and he stormed back to the home we shared, saying that he had quit. "Good!" I exclaimed. My husband had not ever been happy with this job, and had struggled with how to make it all work. I don't think my reaction was what he was expecting. Frankly, I didn't think they deserved him there.

Luckily, Unocal Science and Technology did. Jeff landed a lab technician job there with lovely salary and benefits which enabled us to buy our first home — a four bedroom bare bones model in Chino, brand spanking new. Shauna ran up and down the long hallway, in love with all this newfound space. And I continued working on my master's degree, now commuting through Carbon Canyon or taking the freeway to get to Cal State. Right about this time, my dad decided to part with his old 1960 Chevy truck with the hydraulic lift gate. We arranged to buy it from him to the tune of fifteen smokin' dollars per month — quite a big deal considering we needed to pay Howard back for the $2,500 down payment he had lent us, and that gigantic mortgage we had taken on. $214 a month?!!??! How were we ever going to keep our heads above water?

During those early years I learned skills I never knew I would need to have. Aside from caring for a child and a home, I had to learn how to budget and how to maximize the small amount of grocery money we had. I needed to figure out how to keep the house as cool as possible during the day and throw open all the windows in the evening. Shag carpet and a new dog added more dimensions to my learning curve. And the kicker was how to live with a man.

From the early days of our marriage through about the first ten years, being frugal was a given. We were on a single income, buying a house, and establishing a budget for the first time. I had lived with friends but had never been responsible for all of the household bills. Jeff had lived for a year with a roommate when he was attending Humboldt College, but his parents sent him money to live on. From $155 a month in rent, we were suddenly paying a $214 house payment, homeowners insurance and property taxes, all of the utilities and grocery bills on our own. For me, this became somewhat of an exhilarating game — how little could we get by in food each month? Where were the best bargains to be found? Is it a good idea to continue getting the local newspaper if we get more coupons in it that we can use at the supermarket? We got into gardening, food preservation and canning, both traveling to pick fruit and maximizing the small plot of land we had. I learned to bake bread and goodies, to cook for a small family, and to stretch our food dollars to the limit.

Along with all this were the costs involved in dressing two little girls. So Jean taught me how to select and follow a pattern, and how to choose appropriate materials for a given garment. She and her mother-in-law, Molly, made some cute dresses for the girls, and I pitched in as well, including nightclothes and bathrobes. Toys for the kids were selected carefully and from the cheapest source we could find. After Jeff built his greenhouse, I saved the ends of the two-by-fours and other discarded woods, then sanded them for the girls to build with.

Instead of trips to theme parks, we went to municipal parks and went camping. We rented movies or went to the drive-in. Jeff built the girls a playhouse so they could enjoy hours of make-believe in their own backyard. There were excursions to the beach carpooling with other families, and we brought picnic lunches. Naturally, I worried about everything they might be missing out on because of our choice for me to stay home with them. But to this day, both girls report that they had wonderful childhoods filled with friends and fun.

Over the years, we saved probably thousands of dollars on household repairs and extended warranties because Jeff took care of everything himself. He never ceased to amaze me with not only what he already knew how to do, but also with what he was willing to learn by doing. No matter what the appliance, no matter the plumbing or electrical issue, he was capable of fixing it. Car repairs are included in that list. Of course, he had been a major partner in rebuilding two cars before I ever met him, so I shouldn't have been surprised at his automotive expertise.

To earn some extra money I occasionally babysat – first, for a mom down the street who worked as a nurse, and then, when Shauna was about to start third grade and Jeremie was in kindergarten, I took in another kindergartener whose mom taught at our school, and the infant son of the second grade teacher, Sally, all my kids wound up having at one time or another. Midyear my sister-in-law, Jeff's sister, Diane, had a son, and I watched him two days a week.

It got fun mid-morning. Each day I would take Michael, the second-grade teacher's son, to Marshall School so she could nurse him during recess. With two babies in tow, things would get interesting, especially if it was raining. During lunchtime Sally would bring home the kindergarteners, who were on half-day schedule, and she would have lunch with us and nurse and change Michael. At the end of the school day she would pack everything up and bring Shauna home to me. It was a very busy year, but one of the major benefits was that Sally and I developed a nice relationship that lasted for a very long time. My son and her next child, a daughter, were good buddies. Frequent summer trips to the beach in her van were a treat.

At home, Robin and I would sometimes load up the kids and do the grocery shopping together. Robin and Dave owned a gigantic dragon wagon which fit all of us and all of our families' food needs for a week. At other times we would load up my old Chevy truck with castoffs, pile the babies into the truck and head off to the dump. When my son came along, this was his favorite activity.

That truck also came in handy for recycling projects for the school. Every Friday I would take the truck to the school and parents would throw newspapers in the back, glass bottles in the cab. Sometimes there weren't so many to justify a run up to the recycling center, so I would just leave the truck loaded in the driveway til the following week. Unfortunately, one day we had a gullywasher, rare for our area, and the newspapers got soaked. I hadn't realized how much water paper could retain until I made that next run. The truck wobbled and swerved no matter how much I hung onto the steering wheel. I averaged less than twenty miles an hour on the way to the recycling center. Offloading the soggy newsprint was problematic as well. The helper there that day indicated they couldn't use the paper at all, but would go ahead and pay me because they knew the money was going towards kindergarten field trips. When I drove the truck back over the *scale, I was stunned to discover that I had been making that poor vehicle carry over a thousand pounds of useless newspaper.*

I used tarps after that.

I had always volunteered in my daughters' classrooms, from pre-school on, but once Jeremie hit first grade I had more time on my hands. Linda Norman, her teacher, once told me as she listened to me work with a reading group, "You know, they'll pay you to do this." That was the impetus I needed to start substitute teaching.

Another friend of mine, Paula Bell, whose daughter was in Girl Scouts with Shauna, started subbing as well. By the end of that year we were convinced that this was the career for us, and we applied to Cal Poly Pomona's teaching credential program. For the next year we took core classes together, subbed, and then did our student teaching. I applied for a cutting-edge program that involved a joint-funding agreement between the college and a few school districts. The district would pay four hundred dollars a month to a student who agreed to stay with a school for an entire school year, as opposed to the semester normally required for student teaching. I jumped at the chance to enter this program since it would pay a babysitter to pick up my girls after school and watch them until I got home.

My student teaching year was hell. I got a master teacher who was lackluster at best, and who bad-mouthed me to other colleagues behind my back while giving me little authority in the classroom. Luckily, I had already had some teaching experience and knew I was going to be OK with or without her mentoring. What was even more fortunate and life-changing was that I immediately got placed at my kids' school taking a semester-long maternity leave for a second grade teacher.

Having my own class was tough. All of the responsibilities were, at times, overwhelming. However, in my pod were three other teachers, including Sally, who were always willing to explain what I didn't understand and help out with classroom management when it came up. Dealing with parents was another issue I hadn't had much experience with, since my master teacher hadn't kept me in the loop. It was a bit perplexing the time I sent a detention slip home with a boy from Hong Kong and the envelope was returned with a five dollar bill in it.

I had planned to take Sally's class in the Spring while she went on maternity leave with her next child, but over Christmas break I got a call from the gal I was subbing for, Laurel. This was her first baby, and it was taking more time than she had thought to adjust. Would I be willing to job share with her for the remainder of the school year? The principal and Sally agreed, Sally got another friend to take my place, and suddenly I had a contracted career with Chino Valley Unified School District. This was a good thing, since I had discovered just before Laurel's phone call that I was pregnant with Jeffy. Now I would get the medical coverage and the maternity leave and not lose income.

Our son was born at a birth center in August of that year, 1985, in the presence of his dad and sisters, with aunt, grandparents and Sally in attendance. (She moonlighted as a cake decorator and had made a lovely birthday cake, hovering over the name space until we knew what we had gotten!) Jeff's attitude on this third, unexpected child (conceived on Pearl Harbor Day when I lost track of time) was similar to the other two pregnancies, but all that changed the second he saw his son. Jeff loved his daughters, but having a son brought a new dimension to his parenting. My husband had never really thought of himself as a sexist, but it was clear that his relationship with Jeffy was going to be different from his interactions with his girls.

Laurel and I continued to job share, taking one another's maternity leaves and sick days, for several years. We each worked two to three days a week and were able to continue our volunteer work, keep our houses clean, do all our own cooking — we had it all. Those were the best times of my life. I felt in control and on top of the world. And having the chance to work alongside such a compassionate and competent professional brought my own teaching prowess to new heights.

During this time, Jeff was gaining respect at Unocal in the Science and Technology division. He quickly became known as a lab safety expert, and had a very sensitive nose, which made it easy for him to identify potential hazards with the ventilation system. Though his B.A. was in Biology, he transitioned easily into the world of Chemistry. He had changed from working second shift to days, which had worked out wonderfully when Shauna started school. All in all, this was a smooth period for us.

Shauna gained much confidence entering junior high. She joined drama class and cheerleading and began to add new friends to her group. She had enjoyed a stint at softball as well. In high school she continued in drama, lettered in that and in swim team while keeping her grades up. Shauna had never been one to need much supervision, especially over school work, and rarely asked for assistance. From day one, she was an independent individual. She began to plan for college, applying at Cal State Fullerton, where her father and I and Jeff's brother and sister-in-law had all attended.

At this point Jeff and I had been mulling over moving back into Orange County where the land values were greater, the schools had better test scores, and Jeff would be closer to work. We priced out many homes there, and then decided we were better off where we were and expanding on the home we had. Also, Shauna would be starting college, then Jeremie three years after that, and a larger house payment might make that difficult. Jeff drew up plans and began work on a two-story double family room to be added on to the back of the house, connected to the dining room and kitchen.

It took three and a half years of our doing it ourselves with a few aspects subbed out, but the rooms were showcases. When the project began, we added blessed air conditioning to the furnace system and replaced the old carpeting. By the time the addition was completed, we felt our house had finally morphed into the place we would want to finish out our working years. The downstairs family room provided a large gathering area away from the kitchen. A media area and reading and conversation nooks spread out in front of a big rock hearth. Oak stairs led to the hobby room on the second floor, where Jeff could work on his hobbies, I could sew, and the camping gear could be stored.

The kids were able to have friends over and not feel cramped. In sixth grade Jeffy began to host LAN parties where all of his friends hooked up their computers together (WAAAAY before wireless) and play games together. They would stay up all night eating pizza, drinking cases of soda and virtually killing each other repeatedly. Thanksgiving and Christmas could be celebrated now with lots of family members and plenty of seating. These home improvements and the garage expansion cost $45,000, far more than the original price of the house. Of course, they all contributed to the ridiculously high price we eventually sold the place for.

Shauna's beginning college meant I needed to begin working full-time. This was a difficult transition for me, and required better time management. I had a tough class that first year, which didn't make things any easier. However, as things normally go in education, you have a bad year, the next one will be stellar. And my first grade team was the best in the business. We worked together daily, shared the burden of struggles and laughed together often. Paperwork and prep was shared around so that it was never the case that each of us had to do all of the different learning levels at once. We also traded students around to limit the range of levels within a given classroom. All of us began to spend more time on the more creative aspects of education and began enjoying it more. We also had an incredible principal during those years, Art Hinojosa, who took over a flagging school and turned it into a show place, a California Distinguished School and Title One Achieving School. Our test scores rose dramatically under his hardnosed leadership. He was an inspirational boss.

I began to work longer hours to meet the challenge. And Jeff lost his job at Unocal when they closed the Science and Technology Division.

Unocal was undergoing some restructuring. A lot of testing tasks began to be subbed out. Finally, it was determined by management that it was cheaper to sub it all out because you didn't have to pay benefits or maintain buildings. Some of the folks from various labs from Unocal got together, obtained the patents to a few products began at Unocal, and formed a new company – Entek. Jeff got on board with them. The company struggled for a year, then tanked. But my husband had a lot of industry skills and initiative. He became a consultant and for five years he managed to bring in some income by working with small companies on lab safety standards. One trip took him to Manila City and Jakarta. But *our reserves began to be depleted. I took on a mentoring job with the school district to supplement our income.*

We celebrated heartily when Jeff finally landed a full-time job. During the time Jeff worked for ThermoFinnegan (occasionally known as ThermoElectron or ThermoFischer) as a customer service engineer, calibrating and servicing chemical lab equipment, his hours varied greatly. His workday began at a little after seven in the morning with voice message and email checks. Sometimes he would discover that he was expected in Las Vegas by lunchtime, at other times someone would be helping him book a flight, to be taken that day, to San Jose, Edmonton or Palm Beach. Perhaps he would be driving a couple of hours to Thousand Oaks. Or he might be instructed to spend the day at home, on the clock, laboring on program updates or time or expense sheets. He very often did not know upon rising where he would be spending that day, or that night, or the next week.

At the outset I told him that if the job became too stressful that I would understand completely if he felt he could not handle it, especially if it was taking a toll on his health. I know he was taken in initially because the job responsibilities, milieu and workdays were so very different from his time at Unocal, where he worked the same hours every day in the same lab with the same people doing the same types of tests on the same materials. Of course there was always the fear that, at his age, he might be viewed as unhireable - a risk, too close to retirement. He found this position a challenge and decided he would do what he could every day to meet it.

Often his weekly timesheet said numbers between fifty and sixty. There were worrisome weeks where they were half that. So the ones with the highest numbers became more desirable.

Meanwhile, I was throwing myself into teaching and mentoring and putting in similar hours myself. Our income soared; sometimes Jeff had to laugh when he began to do taxes at how ridiculous our gross income had become. But despite the fact that we slaved back to back in the den at separate desks — Jeff doing expense reports and learning new skills for his job, me grading papers and tests and doing endless lesson plans — we seemed to be drifting apart. Free time found us in separate rooms, we went to bed at different times, sometimes in different time zones, we threw dinner together at the last minute, sacrificing our health, and neither one of us appeared to care all that much if things continued that way or not. We didn't fight. But we also didn't talk much, and, when we did, it was about mundane things.

It might have been partly due to the fact that we were down to one kid at home, and he was, in general, pretty low-drama (except for the car crashes). It could have had something to do with the amount of time I needed to spend at my parents' home as their frailty increased. But we became complacent about our slowly deteriorating relationship. Lovemaking got to the point where it was perhaps monthly, usually instigated by me, and a greater chore each time. We drank more often.

Orange italics which clued in my chat buddies that nookie was imminent were used less and less frequently. The rust-colored satin peignoir remained folded in the drawer.

I was hearing from friends and colleagues that same sense of uncaring division in their relationships. So I wondered if perhaps this was a normal phase in a longterm relationship, and that we would feel closer later on, perhaps upon retiring. Daydreams about how relinquishing the responsibilities and schedules jobs had thrust upon us became more frequent for me. The concept of creating one's own agenda increased its appeal.

Each evening I come home, check for messages on the computer, make some phone calls, eat something forgettable and crash. I pull in the mail from the mailbox on the street if Jeffy hasn't and rifle through it, making certain there aren't any overdue bills. It is very difficult to turn off my racing brain and get some sleep. There is always the nagging thought that something will happen with Jeff in the night and I won't be there when I am needed. But I have to get out of the ICU and the hospital waiting room, because there is no sleep for me there, and I can feel myself unraveling with no rest.

All of the things that used to consume my time in the house – chores, cooking, the remodeling we did, child rearing – retreat to the back ground of my thinking. There is only the here and now, and the here and now is a scary place.

I have very little good to say about Chino. That it was even hotter than the other parts of Southern California was annoying. That our home had no air conditioning was worse. Each summer the temperature would have many days over 110 degrees, and there was little cooling off at night. The arid climate meant that you could knock someone out just by walking across the room to shake his or her hand. It also meant bad hair unless you used a lot of product. If your hair was long, say, waist length like mine was, that meant that it got blown around a lot every fall during the Santa Ana winds – hot winds off the desert east of us, winds that gusted to over sixty miles per hour and blew sparks around which annihilated thousands of acres of forest land and many houses every year. That dryness and heat also made it so it was difficult to sustain decent landscaping. Flowers wilted by ten in the morning. You could water your garden every day and it would still die. Putting in a new lawn required vigilance and a hell of a lot of gallons of water. And what the climate didn't kill the gophers would eat.

But this was where we could afford a house which was still close enough for Jeff to have a short commute, so we made the best of it. We DID have a garden, front and back, and Jeff enjoyed growing a small orchard with a variety of fruit trees, as well as a grape arbor along the back fence. He also designed and built a fully functional greenhouse with better temperature control than we enjoyed in the house.

We got very little rain in Chino, and then once every ten years or so we got a gully washer that had abandoned cars littering the streets. The drainage systems were ill-designed and could never keep up even with lighter rains. Many parents at my school seemed to pay little heed to weather reports, so occasionally we would be slitting garbage bags to throw onto kids who had to walk home. On more than one instance we had to keep children at the school until someone could come to pick them up because allowing them to walk home in hazardous conditions was unconscionable. With many parents having long commutes far from Chino, latchkey kids were the norm, unfortunately.

Winters we would see a few nights below freezing, and then no one would understand how to drive in that the next morning. Saw that sometimes even with just rain. Also, most folks were unaware how to save their plants in freezing temperatures.

There were some lovely areas around us, however. In the foothills or mountain areas you could spot some greenbelts, especially in the spring. The mountains got snow most winters, which was great for taking the kids up to for sledding, and Jeff enjoyed cross-country skiing as well. A few of the older towns valued their ancient trees, and their streets had incredible leafy canopies which shaded the residents from the intense summer heat. But, for the most part, it was the brown you would see – brown grass, brown in the sky from the metropolitan smog that blew in every afternoon with the bit of ocean breeze, and brown trees choking in the heat and pollution.

I used to love the day after a storm, because that meant, as Jeff would say it, "They've moved the mountains back in!" The smog would have dissipated so you could finally see that you really did live in a bowl.

Occasionally an electrical storm would light up the sky to the north of us, with lightning playing against the mountains. We would sit on the brick planter wall surrounding the oak tree out front and watch the display, cheering for the brightest moments. Of course, that would inevitably lead to more forest fires when the bolts hit a tree and the tinder-dry timber exploded.

In terms of demographics, we were in a somewhat different arena from Orange County, or the part of Los Angeles County Jeff had lived in. We were probably lower middle class, with several minorities, at least half Hispanic, and the attendance area of my elementary school, which my children also attended since it was two blocks away, contained some barrio kids who were bussed up from downtown Chino. The plan, devised decades before, was to break up gang activity by ensuring that the children in that area attended different elementary schools, block by block. For the most part, it worked. By the time I retired, seventy-five percent of the students at my school were on free or reduced lunch, and a quarter of them were limited English speaking. My school also housed, from time to time, special day classes for children who were educably mentally retarded, aphasic, or learning disabled. Some of the students who had been determined to be gifted had families who chose to keep them at our school, but some were also attending classes at GATE magnet schools in our district. So, as you can see, we ran the gamut on learning levels at Marshall School — which was both a blessing and a curse. Certainly somewhat of a curse after No Child Left Behind took effect.

We were blessed with an outstanding principal during my tenure there — not for all of it, unfortunately for us, but for a good portion of it. This man brought about many changes in our school and the community in an attempt to take our kids as far as they could go. Included in this set of changes was a program to help parents learn English and how they could help their kids at home. Another program taught by the speech teachers let preschool parents in on what skills they could be working on with their children now to get them ready for our academic kindergarten. Less adept readers' parents had monthly sessions on how to better assist their children at home to help them advance in language arts. Had it not been for this visionary, I don't know that my school and its students would have experienced anywhere near the growth they did.

Other demographic information — we had a highly visible Christian population, with large proportions of Catholic, Mormon and protestant congregations. Most of the houses and apartments in our area were occupied by families with children, with a few retired folks sprinkled around. Many of these retirees were original owners of their homes. My street, in particular, had many families who were the first owners of their homes, just like us. But the remainder of the population was quite mobile. The mobility rate at my school at least doubled over the years I was there. This eats away at student success rates, as well as making them harder to measure.

Politically, Chino was fairly conservative, which is also a function of the high rate of right-leaning Christians living there. Being a flaming liberal tree-hugging rainbow granola eater, this kinda rankled. I had a few sympathizers at my school, but the conservative demographic held there, too. My next door neighbor used to chortle that we cancelled each other out at the polls.

After Shauna moved up to Washington with Ward, we came up to visit – first, for her college graduation, and then for their wedding. We then began driving up here every chance we got – every week and a half vacation we had. Sometimes I would fly up on my own when my school went to the year-round schedule and I had times off Jeff couldn't take advantage of. We fell in love with the area immediately, mainly because of all the things here that Chino was not.

Bellingham is green. No, really. It is green all the time because of being populated by far more fir trees than people. Of course, in order to get the green you have to put up with a great deal of rain – probably three times the annual rainfall compared to Chino and vicinity. But most of the rain fell gently, a light rain, rather than inches a day. The rain let up for a few days each week in the summer, but you could go for weeks even then without having to water your garden. And in the summer the high temperature might be 74 on a given day, compared to thirty degrees above that in Chino. The air is pure and clean, as is the water. And the attitude of the people here is to conserve that.

This is a liberal community. There are a lot of aging hippies here, college kids, and most folks are polite and friendly. We noticed that immediately when driving, because people don't block driveways, for the most part, and wave you in if you are waiting to merge. The demographics, although mostly white, contain a mixture of elements in the minorities, and native peoples abound – smaller tribes, and many of them.

The schools appear to be inclusive of their students with needs, which certainly reflects the national view. Once when I helped out in my oldest grandson's, Zach's, class I saw perhaps a quarter of the kids as having special needs which would have placed them, in Chino, in special day classes. Having a wide range of student abilities doesn't seem to faze the classroom teachers here. And the kids with physical or learning disabilities were valued by the teachers, in front of all the kids. Everyone had a place and was needed there. I was really pleased to see Zach in such an inclusive environment, being in an environment where he would see all of the variation of abilities and disabilities he would find later on in his community as a grownup.

It's way different here. And it's my kind of different.

The Fourth Night

I updated my website with this entry:

Again, thank you for everyone who has commented on the previous entries. You people keep me going.

So, that cough Jeff had for the last two weeks was pneumonia. It wasn't allergies, nor a cold. That bacterium is the suspected culprit that lodged in the blood vessel of his brain, causing a blister. Add high blood pressure and you get what happened Saturday night - brain bleedout. Were it not for the paramedic crew acting so quickly and being so forthcoming with data for the local hospital, that hospital staff assessing the information and calling for the medevac helicopter to land at the park, which happens to be across the street from our house, and directing the paramedics to go directly there, and for the wonderful neurosurgical team and nurses at Arrowhead Regional Medical Center, I would be talking here about funeral arrangements.

Instead, today I got to once again watch my husband reaching out, dangling IV lines everywhere, to touch imaginary dials over his bed, then say, "What the heck is THAT?" to the large imaginary lice he saw crawling on the opposite wall, and to stand over him, hand planted gently on his chest, for a full hour talking him out of getting out of bed. Finally I asked the nurse, Rory, for a suggestion. Not only was Jeff getting a little agitated, but his blood pressure was also a bit over 160 due to our having to argue about his remaining in bed. Even pointing out all the IVs meant nothing. He would forget within a minute or two why he wasn't allowed to get up. Well, I like the way Rory thinks. His suggestion, initally, measured 2 mls., followed by another 2 half an hour later. I was able to leave knowing my husband was now relaxed enough to close his eyes and block out the hallucinations, getting the sleep he so desperately needed at this point, and Rory could also check on his other patient.

Hey, the *Return of the Sith* novelization was very good. Impressive, most impressive... even when read under the conditions I was in for the last couple of days.

The hallucinations which are part and parcel, it seems, of ICU psychosis are hard to reason away. Jeff knows, intellectually, that he is in a hospital, so it is unlikely that gigantic lice, geckos or other infestations would be crawling along the joist of the wall and the ceiling. However, with his short term memory loss, he keeps forgetting this. Many times today I had to physically and verbally stop Jeff from trying to get out of bed to fetch some Lysol or other chemicals, which he was sure would be under the sink, to spray the creatures and get rid of them. At one point I could literally see Jeff's thought processes restart behind his eyes as the conversation we had just had about the critters faded away. And it didn't matter if I took off his glasses (he was suffering from double vision, so the glasses weren't all that helpful), because the fantasized vision would remain. When different therapists come in and remove his restraints, they often forget to replace them, or think they are no longer needed. It seems to me that so long as he is conscious, the straps are necessary for his safety. Finally, his agitation becomes enough to entice the attendants to sedate him.

Since Jeff is sleeping a lot at this point, I sit in a chair next to his bed and read or write. I brought the novelization of *Return of the Sith* along with me to the hospital, and it proves to be an engaging and a quick read. I am glad to have also brought along my yellow writing journal, since it provides a handy place to pen a speedy review. I snake one arm through the slats of the bedside and hold his hand as I read.

Return of the Sith book review written May 17, 2005, while Jeff lay sleeping.

Although read under perhaps the worst of circumstances, this novel was still riveting. I found the style to be quite refreshing, far afield from most of the Extended Universe novels which, to me, are repetitive and pedestrian. Gone are the lengthy and overtold battle scenes. In this novel we connect utterly with each of the major players. I felt as though I understood the motivations, emotions and thought patterns of all of my (now) favorite characters. I especially enjoyed each brief departure from the plot as the author pulled aside a person from the story and opened him up for us for a moment (I can see this as a zoom-out of the background and a freeze-frame as a narrator dissects the soul), beginning with something along the lines of, "This is what it is to be Obi-Wan Kenobi right now." What a wonderful literary device, used to effectively to remind us that this is a character- and theme-driven piece. Folks, how like our fanfiction! MATTHEW STOVER RULES

Creeping bacteria
stealthy, invasive
infecting alveoli
not enough

New turf
burrowed in the head
brainfood

Ignored the cough
tolerated the headache
avoided the doctor
hotbed for disaster

Denial
can tough it out
no longer

It was pneumonia, that cough. Not allergies. Not a cold. And bacteria that caused
it also may have caused the blister on the blood vessel in Jeff's brain. Combine
that with increasing blood pressure brought on by job stress and dietary indis-
cretion, and you have a bleedout.

The longer this goes on, the more I worry about how much of Jeff will
be intact. So far there doesn't seem to be any weakness or loss of mobility, but what about the diabetes and hypertension? Will he be able
to return to work, or to enjoy the activities that filled his days before?

There's a really nice photo of Jeff and me halfway up a small rock formation, leaning back against the rocks, hugging and laughing. I think Brad took it. We were at Joshua Tree National Monument in the high desert of Southern California, probably in the late fall or perhaps winter. I know it must have been a cooler month, because that was the kind of weather we had dressed for — jeans, long-sleeved shirts, and Jeff has on a short jacket, probably the tan denim one he loved. The photo was finished in sepia, which adds to the flavor of the piece. We were young — maybe still in our twenties, or perhaps early thirties. It was a beautiful day, as I recall.

Camping and hiking were things Jeff loved to do. He could go forever, having good stamina and strong muscles. And Jeff was all about the outdoors, having a degree in Biology. He understood what was going on all around him and had a deep appreciation of life. He wasn't concerned about getting bitten or injured, possibly because he knew enough to be respectful of all lifeforms, but also because he had a very high pain threshold. Injuries didn't stop him.

Hiking was something I could get behind, so long as we didn't make a lot of elevation gain and we got back to the campsite at a reasonable time to relax for a few minutes and start dinner. Also, I preferred to use at least a pit toilet and have a place to wash my hands while on the trail. And a shower every morning was essential

Yeah, I pretty much sucked at camping.

My parents never took me camping, so I had no prior experience at it. I never could sleep on the ground, and didn't do that well in a cot, either. There were so many different noises at night. I could never get warm enough once the sun went down. I worried about animals coming around our campsite. Pots and pans never seemed to get all that clean after having been used over an open fire, or even a Coleman stove. And what are you supposed to do with leftovers? Dust and leaf litter got into everything. I HAD to take a shower and wash my hair every morning. Bathrooms are a must. The kids got absolutely filthy before it was even lunchtime.

Hiking? Pretty nice if on marked trails with little rise and perhaps a three-mile loop. I enjoyed the scenery and Jeff explaining things about the flora, fauna and geology of the area. Also good if in partial shade and no rain. But if my husband had his way we would be roughing it big time, in the outback, with frame packs containing all of our needs on our backs and making a campsite out of any semi-flat terrain.

So that is what he did with his brother. Jeff and Brad would go on wilderness hikes, scrambling up rock-strewn mountainsides, heading up past the timberline. Over time, they collected all of the equipment they would need to sustain themselves for several days, upgrading as they saw fit. Using catalogs and each other for references, they sought out the most lightweight, efficient items for their long hiking experiences. They compared prices, weights and lofts of sleeping bags, finally deciding to make their own. Brad began to take this effort to an art form, drilling holes in the handles of titanium spoons to reduce their weight. This, truly, was their major hobby, and it took money and effort to support it. On the other hand, they took care of what they did purchase, cleaning and storing it all away until the next outdoor extravaganza.

Brad took an interest in rock climbing, and that required a whole different set of equipment. He became an expert, teaching a class at a local community college in rock climbing. For the first session, he gave a slide presentation, showing potential climbers exactly what they would be getting into, and how high up they would be dangling. Usually the next class had half the participants of the first, and everyone was ready to get down to business. Jeff didn't involve himself much in this endeavor, preferring to keep his feet on the ground — and that was just fine with me.

Eventually, the brothers began to up the ante. Hiking further and further up into the foothills became scrambling up rocks on mountainsides and, of course, mountain climbing. Brad, when on vacation, would strive to climb all of the Rocky peaks. For Jeff, remaining in California, the goal became to climb Mt. Whitney.

This is no frivolous pursuit. Mt. Whitney is the highest peak in the lower 48. Over 14,000 feet tall, it is craggy and imposing. The weather up there is rarely conducive to the twenty-two mile climb. Staying at the peak overnight is not a good idea, due to the winds and cold. It is not uncommon for a sudden blizzard to occur in the middle of summer. The easiest way up is to travel to Whitney Portal, walk up to the base camp and spend the night, then get up at three in the morning and see how the weather looks — in the dark. If it's dry, it's time to climb. Off you go, and you're back in one piece, hopefully, early in the afternoon. Up, take a picture, down.

Thing is, you have to get a wilderness permit to even try it. So you go online early in the morning in the late spring and start trying to get your permit for the window of time you can take off your job. If you're lucky, that doesn't take you all day. Then you make your plans, pack all your stuff, and drive to Lone Pine. Get up to Whitney Portal, to base camp, and give the hike a try. You get a couple of chances, then your permit expires and you're done for the season.

If the weather winds up being horrible and making the walk too dangerous, you are out of luck until the next year.

Two years in a row, this was the case. They came, they saw, they turned around and came home. Then, in 1990, the third try, Jeff and Brad set out for Lone Pine. That evening, we heard that some horrendous lightning storms set in at the peak earlier that day, and a group of thirteen hikers sought refuge in a stone shelter with a metal roof. Twelve hikers came back down. That same afternoon, another group of explorers took shelter under a huge boulder when the hail and electrical storm made the trail impassable. No one died that time, but all were injured by lightning which was attracted to the iron in the rock.

These terrible reports seemed as unrelenting as the Whitney storms. Unfortunately, Donna, Brad's wife, and I couldn't contact Jeff or Brad, since they had no cell phones, which were just catching on back then. All we could do was pray that they had spoken to the rangers and knew of the dangers they were walking into. The man who had been killed in the hut was wearing glasses with metal in the frames. Both Jeff and Brad wore thick glasses. And most of the other men in the hut were injured, some severely.

Two days later we got the call we had been hoping for. The guys had taken all precautions, had gotten up in the middle of the night and started hiking up the mountain, and had returned to their campsite before all hell had broken lose. Finally, they had conquered Mt. Whitney! Shauna created a celebratory t-shirt in Jeff's honor, showing him climbing up the side of the mountain past the years he hadn't made it to the top.

With our son hitting first grade in the early nineties, Jeff and I got involved in Cub Scouts. Once Jeffy was old enough for camping, his dad offered to help out on every outdoor event. Eventually, Jeffy made Boy Scouts and the camping and hiking escalated. Central California, Catalina Island, and the mountains near San Bernardino held Boy Scout camps that our troop spent a couple of weeks at nearly every summer. And with living in Southern California, there really aren't any seasons you can't spend a weekend camping out.

I managed to avoid most of these events, focusing on fund-raising and sitting with parents each month making decisions on outings and scout policies as they affected our little group. But I got sucked in to the fun promised at the annual Needles canoe trip. It was to be a memorable weekend, where all we had to do was set up camp, wait for the kids to come back from their day of canoeing, and then get fed and entertained. It sounded blissful and relaxing. During the day, that was mostly true, as some of us moms brought books to read, took naps or walked around the fairly bleak campground. There WERE bathrooms and showers, but the water was quite awful in its hardness, and our hair looked worse AFTER we washed it. At night, the wind came up, and was incredibly loud and intense, as was the snoring from the tent next to ours. Needless to say, there was no sleep for me that night.

However, the floorshow that night was fabulous. After having canoed all day, the boys did a marvelous job of singing and performing hilarious skits, including their signature "Chow Mein" – a running joke where the skit is being led by a director who keeps changing his mind as to what genre this movie should be aimed toward, so the dialog and blocking are basically the same, but the outcome is quite different. Topical, and right up the boys' alleys.

And a small group of folks whose job it was to feed us did a wonderful job of it. Just as scouts do everywhere, they used the resources to their best advantage and made the most of the environment in which they found themselves.

The second day of canoeing didn't go quite so well. The boys returned very late after having tried to canoe into that terrible wind all day. There would be no floorshow that evening. All in all, it was a decently fun trip, albeit sleepless, but it was to be my last camping experience. From then on, I vowed to rough it in a lodge.

As the scouts hit their mid-teens, many of them went off to high adventure camp. For Jeffy, that was to be in New Mexico, at a place called Philmont, where a fifty-five-plus-mile hike would begin at around 8,000 feet elevation and go up, often, from there. The hike would be of about a week and a half duration, and the boys would have maps and a couple of adults, and be primarily on their own. They would bring whatever they needed. Water and a food drop would happen from time to time if they arrived at the correct location. Everything they had learned in scouting so far would come into play — group dynamics, leadership, perseverance, orienteering, survival skills, respect for nature, and hiking, especially hiking — pacing yourself and pushing ahead to a daily goal. Working through discomfort, when they encountered little shade and strong sun, and when no amount of dry socks would cushion against blisters. Jeff and Brad would be the adult leaders, with Jeffy and Greg, their sons, and some members of each of the younger Parsons' troops.

They started off well, but midway through the hike a ranger jeeped in to meet them on the trail and inform them that the father of one of our boys had died. This man, who had been of great help to the troop, had been ill but had not been expected to pass away this soon. It was decided that my husband would accompany the boy in the Jeep to the base camp to be put on the train back home. And the rest of the boys determined to finish the long hike in memory of the dad of one of their own, with Brad taking over as the sole adult. Their solidarity made the rest of the trek more somber, yet more resolute. A wide-ranging maturing happened to the young men on that trip.

The troop stepped in and helped the young man, who was heading off to community college, and his high school freshman sister, who was a girl scout, get outfitted for school that fall. We took them clothes shopping and obtained some school supplies. I believe some grocery shopping occurred for them from time to time as well.

Jeffy continued to work on scouting until he turned 18. As he was graduating from high school, he was finishing up on his Eagle Scout project, which was to create an emergency bin for my elementary school in case of a disaster, like an earthquake. For this project Jeffy had to gather a lot of information as to what was needed and what was available nearby, secure funding from our PTA, order the supplies, and organize a work party to sort out and manage the supplies and clean and refill the large water containers. Then, of course, there was the written report on the whole venture, with photos to illustrate each step of the way. I think my husband was very pleased to see Jeffy finish up this important work — not only the project, but to earn his Eagle ranking — in part because he himself was unable to get that far. In addition, Jeffy needed to be able to see this long-term of a job all the way through to the end. I have seen his scouting skills at work in many other aspects of his life, even when it wasn't apparent to him.

Once our son was finished with scouting, much of the camping and other outdoor activities died down for awhile. Without someone else to do the planning, the guys vegged out at home a good deal of the time. A few day hikes in the local mountains or up to Ice House Canyon in the Mount Baldy area were all they could muster up the energy and time for. By this time both of the younger Parsons males were in college, and Jeffy was working part-time. And Jeff's hours had increased at work, as well. There was little time left for play.

Even if the hiking part were over, it would still be crucial for Jeff to be able to putter around the house. I think that would allow him to remain somewhat active while I could still keep an eye on him. While I rue the mess than ensues, it certainly leaves a trail for me to follow.

If you live with a tinkerer you learn to tolerate a certain degree of clutter. A lot of it may be items with which you are completely unfamiliar. Rather than keep all projects in the garage until completed, the common tinkerer rarely actually finishes, so the ventures wind up being spread all around the domicile. Weekends, especially, are times when this oozing of tasks into living and sleeping areas occurs. It goes without saying that these incursions into common areas do not clean themselves up on Sunday nights.

Now, this is where my method of handling the putterer is at odds with the manner in which many wives might deal with him. Hoarders, messy husbands, men with ADHD or just busy guys who have a tendency to flit off on to other things apparently often have partners who simply follow along and clean up after them or nag them into submission. When I have mentioned to other women my husband's propensity to get involved with projects and then, shortly after, abandon them or let them stew for a time, they cannot believe that I ALLOW that. My turning the other cheek to my man's occupation of common areas with broken equipment or ship models is greeted with horror or dismissiveness by my peers. They talk to me about Honey-Do lists and cracking the whip. When it comes down to the shared areas of a home, they feel that the woman should do the decorating and the man the upkeep, and that all home improvement endeavors should have a timeline which is strictly adhered to.

The purpose of a dining table, according to most wives, is to provide a nice venue for meals. It is helpful if the square footage of the table ensures adequate elbow room for all likely comers. In addition, ample kitchen counter space is essential for food prep, a place to set a recipe, and an area to store dirty dishes until such time as the cook (usually) has time to clean them all away after each meal. A buffet can offer a flat display surface for seldom-used ceramic wares and crystal. Coffee tables allow space for a drink, perhaps a pair of tired socked feet at the end of the day, the latest couple of periodicals or a nice photo essay, or a laptop while the user trots off for a minute or two to use the bathroom. And a large rock hearth is a beautiful addition to a family room which deserves to be seen as constructed. These flat surfaces are not to be regarded as workbenches.

In a den, which is not on public view, it is still essential to keep paper-related tasks on your business desk organized, stacked or filed in a manner which makes retrieving them a breeze. Also, when the cleaning lady (me) comes around, it would be best not to assume that she would understand how to sort and pile your important paperwork to your liking. However, dusting in a semi-desert community close to the freeway and in a climate where Santa Ana winds periodically flare up, depositing dirt in their wake, is a chore which must be done from time to time. After all, when we first moved here we both began to suffer from bouts of sneezing, which, no doubt, were exacerbated by the hotter, drier climate and larger quantities of dust and airborne allergens. So it would stand to reason that keeping the dust down and removing it as often as practicable would help.

Bedrooms are best for dressing and sleeping, as well as affection and the expected accompanying activities. These are facilitated by keeping the room free of clutter, and certainly boxes of magazines and catalogs. Closets are generally not the best storage area for pressed flowers, notebooks and novelty hardhats. The shoes and boots on the floor thereof are easiest to find when kept in pairs and in neat rows. Also, it is faster to get dressed on a work morning if the trousers used on the job are not racked along with the grease-stained pairs of jeans normally relegated to the days when vehicles are being restored.

If you bring home all of the soap, shampoo and lotion samples from the hotels you visit at least weekly, a system for storing them in the linen closet will be required. Merely stacking them is doomed to failure, especially when both sides of the said closet are stacked with boxes of homemade jam in their canning jars.

Now, when I worked half-time, which I did for the first eight years of my career, or not at all, which was the case the first ten years of our marriage, I had more time to clean closets, organize shelves, clean the house and generally keep the clutter down. More and more, as I was out of the home more and just got flat-out used to it, I fought the piles and dust less and less. I began to protest less often and just clean around Jeff's projects more. Thus, after thirty years of marriage living in the same home, the hoarding had reached the tipping point.

In the garage, of which he had increased the capacity by fifty percent when he added on to the house, we now had dozens of boxes of magazines (Playboy, Model Railroading, Road and Track, Organic Gardening, Smithsonian, National Geographic, Scientific American and more). Many of those collections were twenty to thirty years in duration. There were twelve fish tanks and their equipment not in use, (three employed in the den), hubcaps (incomplete sets) from every car ever owned by any member of Jeff's family, engines for cars and trucks we no longer owned, aTR3A roadster to be rebuilt and a '66 Mustang in a similar state (my dad's old '60 Chevy truck and a Jeep which had seen better days were parked against the garage in the driveway, with the functioning cars behind them towards the street), jar with formerly pickled piranha, now dehydrated, other fish in formaldehyde, hundreds of model kits not assembled, some models covered with dust which at least got started, paints and tools thereof, many desk items, including stationery, lifted from former employers, all college textbooks and some papers, every can of paint opened and partially used for the house in the thirty-plus years we had lived there, a large coin collection, old wallpaper, HAM radio equipment both antique and current, many old mostly non-working appliances, un-named or numbered chunks of wood, hundreds of homeless keys from everywhere, the largest collection ever of greasy, mixed size and length screws, bolts, nuts and nails, beer brewing equipment and wine making equipment and chemicals.

In the garage rafters collecting dust we had long pieces of very dry wood, an antenna, ski poles and skis, old toddler toys, Jeffy's old crib and Jeff's old playpen, all the Christmas decorations, two huge boxes of packing peanuts, old carpet from the first incarnation of floor covering at that house, parts of the old waterbed Shauna and Jeremie had enjoyed, two seatless chairs, half a drafting table, and old bikes with rotten seats and tires.

Jeff's tool collection was rivaled by none. Among them were all the stripped screwdrivers in the world, many, many sets of hand tools, most incomplete and scattered throughout the garage and backyard, handheld power tools of every type, including airtools, a drill press, band saw, table saw, and a welding setup with several tanks. Yet he drooled over the Grizzly catalog with every new arrival.

In the side yards of our home we had a playhouse taken apart and stored on its side as well as old sliders, both glass and screen doors, a rototiller being choked by grapevines, an antique stove, piles of bricks, brush and branches, a castoff radiator, long sections of PVC and steel pipe, and a sandblaster.

Jeff built a lovely storage shed in the backyard, as well as a fully functional greenhouse stocked with overgrown orchids and cacti whose living environment boasted a temperature range narrower than the one in the house. In the shed I noticed a kiln, canning jars (300+), yard tools which belonged there, wet saw, vacuum pump, thing for machining screws, wheelbarrow, miles of conduit, huge spools of wire, wine bottles and their equipment.

Jeff had worked for three years to add on to our home, which had four bedrooms yet no family room. He solved that by adding a double family room, one floor on top of the other, each with its own fireplace. The downstairs one was used as a normal family room, with a nice TV, sound system that Jeffy helped set up, large hearth, three sitting areas, and an extra dining room table we added to the dining room when we had large family gatherings. Under the stairs was – MORE STORAGE SPACE! This area held a safe bolted to the floor and shelves for homemade canned goods, a wine cellar, and the equipment for making these goods. Meandering upstairs you would find a sewing corner with non-completed kits and projects, a hobby corner for model ship and train building, along with more kits and supplies, a stool and special high-intensity lamp, and a computer and business corner which was no longer in use for those purposes but was now a hobby desk. Two file cabinets and a long closet were also in that space. The cabinets were stuffed with important business documents and old office supplies, and the closet with a huge amount of camping gear – stoves, tents, sleeping bags, clothing, dehydrated food, cots, tarps and more. Overhead a large glider and a few dinosaur models hung, swaying when the fan was on.

None of this made any sense to my neighbors or my friends at work. My parents, when they visited, shook their heads and focused on pleasant conversation, working hard not to comment on the rubble. Me? Mostly I would just smile and bear it. My husband is a brilliant man who can repair any item he sets his mind to, and he does it for free. The time element is problematic, but the results are good, when they occur. All it costs is parts. The labor? We work that out later.

As I muse how we will fill our time when we both get to return home for good, I think about how food and drink have brought us to where we are. It is clear that we need to alter our lifestyle in several ways. We had already begun to take walks at the park across the street, or up and down the blocks of our small neighborhood, but there would have to be much more than that. Alcohol would have to be limited, which would be somewhat difficult for Jeff, since he was a brewer. And menus would have to be reworked – lower in fat, calories and quantity. Since Jeff already enjoyed cooking when he had the time, perhaps it would just be a matter of retraining him. Ah, but could I also train him to clean up??

Orange-red splatters on the back of the stovetop, drips congealing on the oven door, blobs of unidentifiable organic material on the countertops. And MANY pots and pans on the burners, in the sink, none of them rinsed. Yes, Jeff's been cooking again.

It seemed that ANYTHING Jeff prepared was a BIG PRODUCTION ™. There was never any attempt at a one-pan meal; bowls and mixing spoons littered the area like a bloody crime scene. The kitchen sponge sat silently in its spot, dry as a bone OR gummed up with gooey material that hadn't been rinsed off. Spice containers were strewn across the landscape, some tipped and spilling their contents on the counters in a sweet or savory haze that assaulted the senses.

Sometimes things got a little scary, such as when meats were involved, which was usually the case. A platter of raw burgers would be carted out to the barbeque out on the patio, the meat placed on the grill, then in would come the empty platter to be rinsed in warm water, awaiting the cooked burgers. Or the sponge would be grabbed to wipe down an area which had been used for cutting meat, with only H2O as the disinfectant. And all this from a man who had gotten a degree in biology and had won safety awards at his lab and taught lab techs in other countries how to keep their workers from inhaling bad stuff or spilling acids on their skin.

I don't recall any of us getting sick from his daring excursions into salmonella land, but it was all a bit disconcerting. I surreptitiously intervened from time to time when I could — hot soapy water and a clean plate, normally. Heck, I was almost always the clean-up crew anyway, when Jeff cooked. Honestly, I didn't mind so much, taking care of the messes he made. Better him cooking than me, in those days.

Jeff's cuisine was outstanding. He not only attempted food events I would not have tried, but also everything came out fabulous. His lasagna was the best I ever had, with everything but the pasta prepared from scratch. The chili he made was borderline too spicy for me, but worth the extra water I downed with it. He enjoyed making sourdough bread and pancakes, using his own starter. The pomegranate jelly was a trial to remove from the non-jar receptacles, but he liked it. Home-canned vegetables and jams were found only at our home, and the neighbors marveled that ANYONE did that anymore. He had a special zucchini pickle recipe that took up many of the giant specimens he grew in the backyard (my special zucchini bread recipe took up the rest — 48 loaves in the freezer one summer). So we had all the canning equipment, and you know men…once they find another source for tools, which are their toys, look out.

Once he got involved with scouting with our son, more and more cooking implements took up storage space in the kitchen, garage and linen closet. Cast iron became a new material he hadn't really gotten into before, so we gathered cast iron skillets, griddles, hush puppy cookers, and a Dutch oven. The latter could be buried in the ground and used to prepare stew and many other delights, including peach cobbler. Boy Scouts are always prepared, right? So we became prepared to get bowed down under the weight of all that cookware. And we accrued even more fascinating recipes and methods of food prep from the unlikely source of an organization for kids.

Our oldest, Shauna, got involved in cake decorating, which brought about yet another collection of baking equipment, including cake molds and frosting tips. Then that same instructor, Sally (who was also a Marshall teacher who wound up having all of my kids) taught the kids how to make sugar Easter eggs – the kind with a plastic window so you could see a scene within. Jeff got involved with that project in a big way, and we wound up inviting kids from around the neighborhood one Easter vacation to each make a sugar egg project to display that Sunday. If it could be perceived as structural or project-based, Jeff was all over it. Messy? Even better.

Holidays brought out special recipes we never used at any other time of the year. Ordinarily we had a large roast turkey for Thanksgiving and then again for Christmas, inviting his family over to share it all. (My family was never into turkey all that much – we had other traditions we followed.) Jeff would take charge of the bird and its contents; I would sous-chef for him, chopping up the vegetables, opening cans of broth and stirring. I also helped with basting. His stuffing recipe would vary; eventually it contained wild rice and cornbread, as well as dried bread cubes, onion, sautéed giblets, celery, chicken stock, eggs, and a variety of spices Jeff would grind up in his big, strong hands over the huge mixing bowl. The day before the event he would be making pies from scratch. Ones that found their way to the holiday table would be at least one pumpkin, often with the Halloween leftover Jack-o-lantern, a type of fruit such as apple, peach or, the usual, mixed berry his sister found to be orgasmic. (No, really. Those were the sounds she was making.) One Christmas he tried his hand at a truffle loaf with boysenberry sauce that was so rich and thick all you could do was hold it in your mouth and moan. (Unbeknownst to us, my dad had also secretly decided to create a mint truffle pie for dessert that year. I don't think any of us slept that night.)

As in most families, both partners bring their own holiday traditions to the table. Decorating, celebrating within or without a religious overtone, gift-giving and food all either compete or blend over the first years of a marriage. The Liles Christmas tree was artificial, looked the same every year, with every ornament in its place and a train chugging away around its base. The first one of those fake trees I remember was the white plastic Douglas fir-type, with giant spaces between the branches, and only pink bulbs hanging from those sparse fronds. The Parsons might not have a tree, or it might go up just before family arrived, but it would be fresh-cut or living. The Liles décor was like the cooking – both quantity and presentation were key. Parsons décor was more sparse, because it took time they wanted to devote to other endeavors. Liles cards went out just after Thanksgiving. The Parsons might send them a couple of days before the event, if at all. While the tree at our house was real, we generally put the same decorations in the same places each year, and there was a train involved from time to time, since Jeff was a hobbyist. Our cards went out by the middle of December. Jeff and I felt we brought equal parts of our upbringing to our holiday times. And that was best reflected in the baking.

My mom had been brought up in Nebraska on a farm where, as her mom would say, "We cook for thrashers" (she meant threshers, and other itinerant farm workers). Quantity was first and foremost, and with Christmas cookies, it was variety, and huge quantities therein. We had every type of chocolate-peanut combination imaginable, including O'Henry bars, buckeyes and both chocolate and peanut butter fudge. But the thing our family was best known for was peanut jumbos.

Imagine, if you will, a vanilla or yellow sheet cake left for a day or two to cure. Now cut it into squares – perhaps twenty-four of them. Encase each of those on all sides with home-made vanilla frosting, and then roll them in finely chopped peanuts. Simple. Deadly. Teen-agers left in charge of making these have a high failure rate, since the cake chunks want to crumble under normal handling, and eating several of these failures can result in "peanut poisoning" – something which ruins any attempt at a dining experience for days. Trust me.

My husband's family had their own baking traditions, including a few Danish items. Kringler, a pretzel-shaped buttery sugar cookie which is somehow simultaneously light and rich, has never been duplicated properly outside of my mother-in-law's strict supervision. School cookies, misshapen large, flat cookies replete with chopped dates and/or currents, were always my husband's favorite, but since the rest of us weren't that enamored of them, they were always the last Christmas cookies remaining as we approached New Year's. Jeff was not a big fudge fan, but he helped stir the stiff concoction when the molten sugar needed to be combined with the mostly unsweetened chocolate and marshmallow crème. If my dad talked me into it, there would be his favorite chocolate chip cookies made with half whole wheat flour, honey or maple syrup but no white sugar, and a variety of chips and nuts. A few bar types found their way onto the holiday plate as well.

For us Parsons, the Christmas goodies provided a whole 'nuther exercise in how to destroy a kitchen. The added double-threat of airborne flour dust and gritty, sticky sugar of TWO TYPES, potentially even HONEY (in warm Southern California where ants are just WAITING for the siren call of sucrose) meant I was cleaning more often than cooking. And then if you add children decorating cookies, getting the frosting and colored sprinkle sugar on every surface imaginable, including themselves, you have the means to a meltdown – a Mommy meltdown. One particularly busy baking time, when I hadn't stopped to clean up for a couple of hours, my parents-in-law walked in for their weekly visit. I held my breath as my mother-in-law surveyed the scene. One never knew how she or her husband might react to our being in the middle of things when they arrived. Jean's eyes traveled over the splattered children and countertops, the reams of waxed paper and foil sprayed with *baking ingredients and some finished products. For a moment, probably the first moment of the day, there was a hush over the ruined kitchen (my perspective). Finally, Jean threw up her hands as her husband munched appreciatively on one of the baked goods. "Such activity!" she declared in admiration, reaching for an apron. I should have known. This was probably pretty close to how it looked at her place when her kids were little. After all, Jeff had learned from the best.*

I adored my mother-in-law that day for having said that. But I really shouldn't have been surprised. Homemade was best; homemade cookies were stellar in her eyes — she was Danish. She pitched in and helped, we cleaned up as best we could and started dinner, and all was well. I was the one who always wanted the house to look nice when they came over; they couldn't have cared less. Jeff knew how they felt and couldn't ever get why I was always so frantic about dusting and vacuuming right before his folks arrived. But he never was a daughter-in-law, was he?

In the end, it was never, for anyone else, about how clean the house was. It was the way it smelled, the wonderful aromas and tastes of a shared and melding holiday tradition, the sparkle of tinsel and champagne, the rustle of wrapping and then unwrapping treasures, the dogs ripping apart the castoff colored paper littering the living room floor. The Liles carefully folding and setting aside the wrappings before they ever could hit the floor: the Parsons wearing removed ribbons and bows as jewelry, raffia tiaras, throwing the tissue all over the place almost as the spoils of all that loot. The fudge, the kringler. The turkey and stuffing, the sirloin tips and mashed potatoes. Christmas Eve, Christmas morning. Carols, movie. Yin/yang. Peaceful coexistence, honoring both houses, taking favorites from both. And wondering in several more generations how our peanut jumbos and Christmas trees would look.

The Fifth Night

I post this on my website the following evening as I await notification of the time that Jeff is changing hospitals. At first I am concerned because the plan is to transfer him the forty-plus miles from Colton to USC by ambulance. What if they get stuck in commuter traffic? This seems like a terrible idea.

This morning I got a call as I was waking up - 6:20. Jeff had stopped breathing.

He is being taken to USC Med. Cntr ICU this evening because he needs a type of surgery they couldn't do at the Arrowhead Reg. Med. Cntr. – a stint installed in the vessel that is damaged and going into spasms. The procedure is called coil embolization.

I will be not here until further notice. Thanks for all the good thoughts.

In the end, they realize that Jeff might be too fragile to make the trip via ambulance and decide to airlift him, so he gets yet another helicopter ride he will be sedated for. Unfortunately, I am sitting at home awaiting this information and am not called until the flight is actually underway, so there will be a gap between the time Jeff gets to the hospital and I finally drive there. In addition, I initially go to the wrong place and have to call for directions, delaying my arrival even more.

Although I feel a lot of trepidation about this move, I am just as happy because a bed was found for him at one of the two hospitals in Southern California that offer this surgery. The way it will work is that they will insert a tiny coil in the leaking blood vessel, and that will slow the seepage until the area is able to heal itself. Keeping Jeff's blood pressure under control will be key now.

The difference between the two facilities is apparent upon driving up to USC University Hospital. Clearly, there is money here. The architecture announces it, the cleanliness reaffirms it, the reception area oozes it – everything about this place begins to relax me. Innately, I realize that with more money, there is likely to be a greater number of personnel taking care of my husband, perhaps a higher level of care and education of the caregivers, and newer, more up to date critical care equipment. I breathe a sigh of relief that I won't worry about having my purse stolen in the waiting room or being mugged on my way out to the car at night. The liberal in me is kicking me for my elitist attitude, but the wife is cheering for a better environment for the husband.

And the really good news is that my daughter, Shauna, is on her way from Washington.

Pregnancy is a strange affair. The number of changes it brings about in a woman's body is probably uncountable. The morning sickness was fixed by meds which are no longer available, since they were deemed to cause birth defects. We were lucky there, I think. However, other issues arose, such as cooking smells causing nausea. Surprising that I was the victim this time. (My cooking skills have only just improved in the very recent past.) My appetite's waxing and waning was pretty much following the clock — not so hungry STARVINGSTARVINGSTARVING yuck. Rinse and repeat the next day.

THEN I got hold of Adele Davis' <u>Let's Eat Right to Keep Fit</u> and I launched into a whole nuther aspect of pre-parenting: questioning everything that went into my mouth, every action I performed, and the quality of every night of sleep. Adele Davis had this strange concoction she recommended preggers drink daily. It consisted of every foul-tasting supplement on the market poured into a blender. One was to drink a quart of it each day. I think it was the zinc powder in there that rendered anything yummy you would add to the mix as metallic on the tongue. But, if I were to give birth to a superbaby, down that crap I would. Most days, anyway.

I went into labor one Sunday late morning in February. Jeff had gone over to his parents' home, but I hadn't felt like going with. Soon I discovered why. Calling him, I told him I felt this was it. He arrived shortly after, and the troops followed quickly — his parents, my parents, his sister and brother, my best friend from high school, Linda, (with camera), his sister's friend…I don't think I mentioned this before, but this was a two-bedroom one-story square converted garage. That was a lot of people to cram in there. Jeff's sister and her friend commandeered the kitchen, where they commenced to baking a "birthday" cake with seven eggs — for fertility. TOO LATE!

After some phone calls, the midwife appeared. Between the time Hubby called and her arrival, I careened into transition — a stage of labor accompanied by hard, frequent contractions, the grasping of the offending one's arm (whoever is near, preferably the one who impregnated you in the first place) and digging in of claws, and general loss of control. All Lamaze instruction flew out the window. There was no breathing technique in place, except the gasping type. So the midwife walked in to Hell.

After several minutes of reinstating the calming, the focus, and the proper breathing for this stage of delivery, taking her measurements ("You're at eight-and-a-half, Dearie — just right! Not much longer now!") and clucking away at me, she put Jeff back in charge and went out to the living room to call the OB. So I am lying there breathing away, thinking we have an hour or two left, that I can do this, and I visualize rolling over the contractions rather than having them bowl me over.

Meanwhile, the doula is on the phone with her boss. My mother-in-law reported to me, months later, that she had been washing the dishes and ironing to keep busy, and had overheard the one side of the conversation which was taking place a wall away from where I lay in the ending stages of labor, completely oblivious.

"GET YOUR ASS OVER HERE RIGHT NOW! I am NOT delivering this child for you. She's already at ten-and-a-half! NOW!!"

Of course, every minute she was around me or Jeff, all was sweetness and light. This was my first child. She could have told me *ANYTHING*, and with my lack of experience in these matters — knowing nothin' 'bout birthin' no babies — I would have believed her.

My good friend was clicking away on a camera with no film in it.

A cake awaited, so Shauna arrived right at dinnertime. Her long, dark hair had been swirling around just outside my vagina, so, between contractions, the midwife and the OB played with it, curling it around their gloved fingers and taking bets on the eventual color. I can't recall who won.

They had forgotten the scale, so the OB just hung the baby upside down and estimated that she weighed eight pounds, four ounces. After his twenty-five years of deliveries, no one argued with his assessment.

She was all eyes, this baby. Big, huge, expressive eyes taking everything and everyone in. They took turns holding her, although my mother-in-law really didn't want to let her go. We have a few pictures of different relatives holding her, staring down at the eyes that just sucked you in.

What began soon after was months of stumbling. I had no idea how to parent children in general, and this baby in particular. I was the youngest. I had little babysitting experience, and all of it with older kids. My mother-in-law was a godsend; I was on the phone to her daily, asking for advice. She gave me her worn copy of Dr. Spock's Baby and Child Care, and although it was terribly out of date, I nearly memorized it. I have to admit I was completely out of my element after having spent four and a half years commuting to both college and work, on the go constantly, mentally alert and nurtured. The only way all that prepared me for parenting was to get me used to surviving on little sleep.

Jeff and I took a rare night off and went to see "The Exorcist". For months I stared at my child, wondering when she would start rotating her head and spewing pea soup.

Now don't get me wrong. Shauna was perfectly normal, except that she was incredibly brilliant, unflaggingly creative and craving stimulation, verbally gifted and gorgeous. I mean, other than that she performed her milestones on time. But I felt absolutely unprepared for the headstrong, independent child she was growing to be. In so many ways I saw both myself and a stranger in her.

I know once Shauna arrives that everything is going to be all right. My strong, intelligent managerial-type daughter jumps in, feet-first, and I no longer feel as though I am facing this traumatic experience alone.

It is one thing to have family and friends a phone call away. It is one thing when they can stop by for an hour or a day and provide me the support I need but had been denying. But when Shauna arrives it is as though the space in my life Jeff occupied – the quiet strength, the bouncer-off of ideas, the person who assures you simply because of their presence that you are part of a couple – can now be filled up by his daughter. Immediately, literally upon seeing her walking towards me, I begin to mold myself spiritually to lie against the sometimes jagged edge of her being. I can never thank this child enough for being who she has become, and for putting her life on hold to bolster her family during this time.

Despite some pull from Shauna and other family members, I strive to keep my daughter Jeremie out of the loop. She is due to deliver a child in three weeks, and I am concerned about how a prolonged visit here at the hospital might affect not only her health, but the baby's. I do keep her updated, but encourage her not to come and visit until we have a better idea of Jeff's prognosis. Perhaps after the coil procedure is performed would be a better time for Jeremie to drive down here from her home in the high desert.

Of course, the natural progression from having an amazing child is wanting another. With each childbirth, I felt calmer and more in control, and my husband seemed to have more fun with it all. As I've described, with our first, having her at home meant we were in charge until a professional got there, so when we lost control of the contractions, there was no one to set us straight, and we reacted accordingly – panic. After Shauna was born, Jeff and I decided that we would circumvent that problem by using birth centers, so long as they worked in accordance with how we felt giving birth should be – not pushing drugs or medical intervention, but rather just providing backup for us, and a doctor and/or midwife just in case.

So with Jeremie's birth, we immediately felt more in charge. We used the same OB, since we had felt comfortable with him as a professional, but went with his birth center delivery instead of homebirth. I remember having no problem maintaining focus on his wallpaper. I recall a great sense of calm and quiet. Jeff's brother was in charge of the camera this time, with Linda being unavailable. But most of the same crew of family and friends were nearby.

We had heard of the LeBoyer method of delivery, and liked some aspects of it. Giving birth in a tub wasn't something we were confident with, so we simply added in the dim lights and quiet atmosphere. However, Jeremie was in somewhat of a hurry. Jeff didn't have time to get from standing near my shoulders to standing at the bottom of the bed to catch her. Brad recorded the moment, with the low lighting, as a reddish blur as she shot out of me – luckily, into the doctor's waiting hands.

Jeff had generally left the vast majority of child rearing decisions to me, probably knowing that I was getting a lot of my information from his mom, anyway. He backed my options and never complained about late dinners or a dusty floor. I recall many cold dinner plates sitting on the arm of the couch as I waited for this second child to finish HER dinner.

Just nursing Jeremie became a full-time operation. I was all for on-demand feedings, but she took it to an artform. However, she stopped it all just as quickly when she developed a stuffy nose due to a cold right after her first birthday. Unable to nurse, and having already been introduced to the cup, she stopped nursing cold turkey. Several days after weening, she pulled at my shirt as I was sitting on the couch calming her for her nap, so I whipped it out. She laughed. End of nurseytime.

Shauna took a fairly immediate dislike to her sister, possibly due to her feeling slightly nauseated at any spewing, drooling or messes, but I fell in love just as hard as I had with the older child. I had had some trepidation before Jeremie's birth, thinking I couldn't possibly love another child as much as I did Shauna, but, as most moms and dads discover, parental love is pretty much boundless.

Between the two arrivals I had earned my Master's degree in Linguistics, attending college part-time while Shauna was bounced between her grandma and her dad. After Jeremie's birth, however, there came a lull in my learning, and a void in my life. At the time it was unformed and undefined; hindsight renders a crystalline view. I was bored. Working around Shauna's preschool schedule of three part-days a week, I baked, Jeff and I canned fruit that we drove out to buy and/or pick, I learned how to sew dresses for the girls, took on the presidency of the PTA, and I began to watch daytime television. This was a bleak episode in my life. Finding out how to zone out alpha waved my brain into accepting the drudgery of being a stay-at-home mom. By the time Jeremie hit kindergarten, winning me back a few hours a week, I started to dwell on something Shauna's teachers had said to me when I helped out in their classrooms: "You know they will PAY you to do this, right?"

So I started substitute teaching after Jeremie entered first grade. Again, there was dissatisfaction. Having students only a day or two at a time never gave me the chance to see growth and change, which I had begun to thrive on watching in my own girls. The mother of one of Shauna's friends and I went back to college together to earn our teaching credentials.

Now, it was perhaps unfortunate that I hadn't noticed a trend in my life: every time I finished a college degree or certification, I became pregnant. As soon as I completed my credential requirements and got a job at my children's elementary school not two blocks from our home, I got pregnant with Jeff (not Junior – he is Jeff, his dad, Jeffrey). Jeremie was our one planned child. Shauna, of course, had precipitated our marriage. Jeff, our third, was a shocker.

I remember being quite tired one late fall evening, but Jeff Sr. was feeling frisky. We were using that time-honored birth control method of the combination of a diaphragm and rhythm. The one from which many children have sprung. My counting was a little off. It was December 7, 1984 – a day which will live in infamy.

After spending the first ten years of our marriage staying at home with the girls, I had just jumpstarted my career in teaching – finished my credential after a year of subbing, did my student teaching, and was in the workforce as a long-term sub, doing a semester for a lovely gal on maternity leave from the elementary school just down the street from us. The girls were able to come into my classroom after their schoolday, help me set things out for the next day, file the finished work, and start their homework. It was a win-win job, but was to be over at the end of January. The teacher whose class I had taken over called me shortly after Christmas, lamenting that motherhood was much more demanding than she had thought it would be, and wondering if I were interested in jobsharing – splitting the school week with me – for the rest of the school year, and beyond, if it worked out. "Well," I responded, "If you'll take MY maternity leave this fall. I think I'm pregnant."

My husband supported this decision fully. He could see that, given half a work-week, I was *able to juggle parenting, volunteer work, a clean house, and baking and cooking. (And the extra income was a bonus!) We prepared for the birth of our third child confidently.*

This child was delivered at a different birth center from Jeremie's due to our decision to go with someone more local. The physician spent most of the monthly exams worrying about my weight and blood pressure, the second of which was always within normal parameters. After finally figuring out that I was not diabetic nor any health risk whatsoever, he agreed to do a birth center delivery. However, his offices WERE just down the street from his contracted hospital, so it was all good, so far as he was concerned.

When we arrived for the delivery, he did the prelims and determined how far along I was, then observed how very much in control Jeff and I were. Since it was near midnight and he had had a busy day, he flopped in an armchair in a corner and went to sleep. I, in the meantime, had discovered that I was uncomfortable lying down, so I paced the rooms, pressing my hands flat against a wall and leaning in with each contraction. We woke the doc up when I lost the mucous plug, always a signal for me that transition was at hand, and pushing would not be far behind.

I had a bit more trouble pushing this child out than I had the others. The OB explained that uteruses get flabby over time and with each successive pregnancy are less resilient. When Jeffy came out, he was a bit blue and shivery. His dad scooped him up in a blanket and disappeared out into the hallway with him quite soon after.

Jeff and I had had many conversations about kids. Some had focused on their gender, and how we might bond differently. He had always insisted that he would love each of his children equally. His son made a liar out of him. From the moment Jeffy was born, his dad was sucked in.

The man who had been perfectly happy to leave the lioness' share of parenting to me gradually turned into much more of a hands-on daddy. Partly it was the child's gender, partly that I was working now, and maybe it had something to do with the fact that he felt more secure as a dad, having had the girls to practice on. But step up to the plate he did, and most of the time I enjoyed the fact that some of that weight had been removed from my shoulders.

For the first eight years of my son's life, I worked half-time, job-sharing with Laurel, a saint of a woman. We took each other's maternity leaves and sick days. I learned almost everything I needed to know about how to be a first-rate teacher from her. And I stuck with the PTA, with volunteer work with Girl and Boy Scouts, continued to bake bread, can, and keep my house relatively clean. It was a most awesome time in my life.

There are quiet moments as Shauna and I settle in to a routine at USC University Hospital. We do take some time to catch up, since Shauna lives in Washington state now, and we only get to see her when we drive up to visit perhaps three times a year. But there are lulls in the conversation. It is hard to do much reading or napping when we are stuck in the waiting room during Jeff's tests and procedures; my mind drifts.

I always had felt that my parents were a bit odd. Our household didn't run like June Cleaver's, and my folks did a lot more playing around than any other adults I saw on TV. Plus, my parents were terribly affectionate, and the adults on TV slept in twin beds. And when it came time for discipline, we got it, which I rarely saw happen anywhere else. When my brother and I had crossed the line, we heard my dad call out, "LINE UP!" and we began to cry and quake.

Those two words struck fear into our cores. We knew we had blown it. My dad slowly removed his belt, and we were to stand bent over, jeans bottoms facing him, and take what was coming to us.

Now here is the part that gets a little dicey for me. I honestly don't recall actually getting hit or feeling any pain. What I felt was fear and humiliation, shame and regret. We made our parents feel disappointed in us. What swats we got (maybe one or two per discipline episode) were pretty mild. No marks were ever left, that I can remember.

My mom slapped me across the face once. I was twelve and had mouthed off. Whatever it was that I had said, I am pretty sure I deserved what I got. I don't recall my mother ever disciplining me physically aside from that one time. She told me she had bitten me once, after I had bitten my brother on the back. That hadn't been the first time I had bitten as a youngster – I was probably three or four at the time. Nothing she had tried would make me stop, so she took my arm and bit down on it. Of course, that was the end of my biting, as the slap also reminded me to think before I spoke.

Jeff didn't tell me much about discipline at his home, but I gather there wasn't much swatting going on. His mom would have taken care of the parenting mostly, since she was at home and Howard at work. Once Jeff did tell me that his mom would get in his face if he misbehaved, and her speech took on an angry hiss. She also was prone to saying things that occasionally bordered on verbal abuse, but it wasn't a daily occurrence. In general, she took the oral approach to discipline – lecturing.

I took over parenting in our new family when I first conceived. I was the one who read the books, who concocted the horrendously awful Adele Davis Superbaby quart of yuck from Hell every day, held my nose and downed it, I who stayed home with the kids for the first ten years, I who got up at night to nurse them and deal with colic, I who worked at keeping them quiet after Jeff got home from work, I who took them to doctors' and dentists' appointments, I who refereed fights. I who pretty much pushed Jeff out of the picture until I began to work full-time and couldn't split my energy like that anymore.

Just so you get the picture. This wasn't orchestrated by Jeff. But he also didn't shove his way back into the scene all that much, either.

My figuring was, the person who was staying home should be dealing with the housework, cooking and parenting. My mom hadn't been able to be a housewife, having had to go back to work when I turned two, but Jeff's mom had never worked a day in her married life, and she was the one I was kind of emulating at that point, calling her daily to find out why Shauna was doing or not doing whatever she was or wasn't doing. We were at Jean and Howard's every weekend. Jean babysat Shauna one afternoon a week so I could go back to college. My parents both worked and had long commutes. I glommed on to the Parsons family in a big way. And so I began to copy Jean in terms of the quantity of parenting that went down at the Parsons'. Having not had the model in my formative years, I found one that worked and did things in that way.

It wasn't easy, doing it all. And it was even harder having no adult conversation or diversion at home. One day of college was awfully nice but not nearly enough. I poured a great deal of energy into working with Shauna but felt empty a good deal of the time. Never having babysat someone so young, I relied on Jean and baby manuals to figure it all out. I knew this was a job you couldn't fix readily if you messed it up. Thing was, Shauna was not a complacent child. She was intelligent and strong-willed. She required a lot of stimulation, could not stand being bored. And until we moved to Chino, there was no other child around for distraction and socialization.

Looking back, I know I watched too much TV, and allowed her too many PBS shows (nothing else). She adored all of them, so it was hard to pick what to let her watch each day. I read thousands of books to her, involved her in art projects and cooking, and we spent Jeremie's nap time with building sets and board games. Both girls attended a YMCA co-op preschool in Diamond Bar – Shauna had started out at one closer to home, but I got disenchanted when there was a change of management – and part of the deal to have your child at the Y was to volunteer time to help out the teachers to keep the adult-student ratio low (1:6). Two- and three-day programs were available, mornings only. There were a good many pre-reading and math skills taught there, as well as the usual singing, outdoor play and a lot of socialization, which I felt was needed to help with a smooth transition to kindergarten.

So even though mornings were busy, after lunch the time seemed to drag. I found myself drawn to soaps, and sometimes a couple of game shows. After I had finished up my master's degree, I felt as though my brain had begun to shrivel, and these people on TV had a heck of a lot of stuff going on in their lives – which I didn't. I even picked up a few romance novels lent to me by my next-door neighbor, who was a real aficionado. Anything deeper just seemed out of the realm of possibility.

But as the kids got bigger and Shauna started kindergarten, things improved somewhat. For one thing, no longer having a tiny baby around meant managing the household was getting easier. Once Jeremie hit preschool, I began to have a couple of mornings to myself during the school year, which I hadn't had for six years. I could do grocery shopping with no kids in tow. Working on housework and PTA responsibilities was more manageable.

But I found out what parenting with no relief, what running a household completely alone was like when the Oil, Chemical and Uranium workers went on strike. As part of management (the Science and Technology Division of Unocal was considered part of management), Jeff was contracted to step in for striking workers. We waited with a great deal of trepidation to find out where in the world he would be assigned. Would it be Texas? Somewhere in Asia? Colorado? In the end, we were relieved to discover that he was only going to be going to Wilmington Refinery, near Los Angeles.

The first night he was gone on strike assignment was very quiet, and very strange. I had never lived alone, so I had never slept in a house with no other adult around. Jeff was told he was to be locked in at the refinery, and would work seven days a week, twelve hours a day. Lovely meals would be brought in — steak, shrimp, all the trimmings — and recent movies shown nearly every night. But they slept on cots in offices. Maybe one night every week or two, Jeff would be able to sneak out after his shift ended and come home, but he had to be up and out, back at the refinery before the strikers returned early in the morning. So a hug for the kids, a little nookie, a few hours for snuggling, and back he went.

What we had thought would be a couple of weeks of strike duty turned into three months. This was a tremendous boon to our bank account — Jeff earned over $7,000 in those three months (and this was back in 1980), and I learned to become more self-sufficient. I had taken on some of Jeff's chores and lived to tell about it. Never a gardener, nevertheless I had to take care of the winter veggie crop, harvesting, weeding and processing the crop. There was a great deal of onion chopping for freezing. I called Jeff and asked him if I could buy a food processor. He was rather stunned I hadn't just gone out and done that. By the second month, I had decided to paint the kitchen, and did it. I was starting to get a little cocky by the time he was allowed to come home for good.

But a couple of years later, when Jeremie joined Shauna at the elementary school, I gave myself somewhat of a setback in that I took on three kids to babysit — two of them infants. The income was wonderful, and I felt that I was contributing, really contributing to the running of the house. For some reason, everything else I had done wasn't enough. That was MY point of view, not Jeff's. Even that year, I never asked Jeff to do any of the housework or cooking. I had divided up the chores by location and skill: I took care of everything inside the house, his domain included the yards and garage and any repair work that was required. After that strike was over, everything had gone back to the way it was before.

But taking on the extra childcare responsibilities meant not enough mental stimulation again. I began to count down the days til that school year ended. With Jeremie in school full-time as a first grader, I would be able to get a job outside the home. I was going to substitute teach.

Fast forward a few years. I was on top of my game in my career, did my PTA and Girl Scout volunteer work, volunteered in my kids' classrooms, worked with Jeffy at home, kept the house clean, baked and canned. Because of working part-time, I could still do everything else, at least to my satisfaction. Jeff had started work on the addition to the house, and Jeffy loved watching what everyone else was doing. He was the easiest of the three kids while he was little.

Because our youngest was his son, Jeff seemed to be participating in parenting a bit more and I didn't mind that in the least. I learned to let go a bit, which teaching also had taught me to do. Being rigid in the classroom simply doesn't work. Most of my life I had gotten by with making plans, crossing things off lists, and carrying through even if things hadn't really gone as planned. It was close to impossible for me to be spontaneous. But in teaching, I had discovered that stuff happens. A kid throws up on a book. An abused child has a breakdown in the reading center. The lights go out as you are instructing a math lesson using an overhead projector. It rains and you can't do the outside P.E. lesson in the next time block. You get a new student. All KINDS of things happen, and it's like that nearly every day. So I learned to be more flexible. And that bled into my home life as well.

The fact that Jeffy was an easy little one and the girls were growing up was helpful, too. My daughters were learning to do some of the household chores and were dabbling in cooking. Eventually we developed a chore chart, with the allowance amounts each job was worth. The kids would choose their jobs for the month. The next month they might want to switch around, or stick with what they had chosen. I took up the slack on whatever got left on the list. Funny, my allowance never seemed to arrive…

Of course, as the girls each entered their teens, parenting them changed. Jeff and I were much more likely to work together as a united front, which actually sometimes was effective.

But there were times…

"Fuck you!"

All three of them have said it, some more than once. But nothing knifes through you quite the way that expression does when spoken to a parent by a child.

Perhaps it's a generational thing. When I was their age, I never heard the word "fuck" ever. It wasn't bandied about in the hallways at school, nor floated across my sidewalks in Westminster. I might have been in college when the word began to take on a life of its own during the hippie Woodstock student protest flag-burning bra discarding 60s. It had a stunning effect then. Voices would become louder when pronouncing it, drawing it out and raising both in tone and volume to deliver the ultimate smackdown of a conversation or an argument. Twitters of embarrassed and enthralled giggles would usually follow. By the time I hit my twenties it was beginning to filter its way into bits of the entertainment industry, in music and movies. Once in awhile a celebrity would utter it, and it would be bleeped over. In my mind, I bleeped it all along. I never spoke it. Unseen pressures from my youth — religion and culture, as well as my own family upbringing — would ensure that.

But there it was, coming out of the soft mouth of one of my children in retribution for some authority I had wielded as a parent. It was spoken partly in anger but also for effect. Trying to remind myself of the commonplace aspect the word had taken on in pop "culture" and its pervasive presence in all aspects of my kids' lives outside the door of our home, I would steel myself from the shock and slap just one step away from an actual physical assault. But the term still had its desired effect. Whether I reacted right there in the hallway or, later, in my bathroom or in the backyard, I would dissolve.

Fuck you. I don't want to hear any more. Stop talking. The child would bring the lecture to a complete halt by enunciating those two little words. And I remained incapable of defending myself against them.

I suppose I was fortunate. I wasn't battered by the offending phrase very often. Now, thinking back, I can't recall a time my husband, their father, was ever assailed by it. But, then, I wasn't the one putting holes in the walls on an annual basis, either. Now THERE was the ultimate conversation stopper.

The Sixth Night

The coil embolization procedure is performed on Jeff, and there are many more tests and therapies done. For some of those, I or we can remain in the room. Sometimes I just excuse myself, because what is being done to Jeff or with Jeff is something I don't want to witness. Other times I think that perhaps as Jeff's next-of-kin I should be on hand to ensure that his dignity is intact, however much can remain in a situation such as this one. In part, that is about whether he would be embarrassed if I were still in the room. (His being conscious or not doesn't seem to matter to me; I think about his need for privacy regardless of his being aware of what is happening or not. Does that seem strange?) Also, if the procedure is something I may need to reproduce later for him at home, I need to learn how it is done properly. So I am there for respiratory therapy, but not for baths. For many tests I am shooed out of the place because either a team is there and there just isn't enough room for all of us, or I am removed for my own safety or sanity. In addition, Jeff is often taken to another area in order for a machine which is stationary to be utilized. So if it is close to what would be a mealtime for me and Shauna, we head over to the commissary on the first floor to scarf up whatever is left – often the times we go make it impossible to create a balanced meal. It is a very small and not well stocked cafeteria. Other times we go outside in front of the medical center to place cell phone calls to loved ones or just soak up a bit of warmth. This hospital is a very pleasant, well-kept facility, and there is no part of it where I feel unsafe, inside or out.

A lot of our time is now spent in the waiting room, where family members come and go. It becomes hard to keep track of what I have told whom. Some folks can handle the flat-out truth, still others need a little sugar-coating. I have to keep that in mind on the phone and in person. The personalities of members of both sides of this family are diverse, as are their education levels and backgrounds.

"You gotta go see the cute chick that works in the soda shop!" A young guy working with my dad at the gas station back in the early forties raved about the girl with a bob behind the counter at the drug store across the street. Eventually my father's teenaged curiosity was piqued, so he cleaned himself up a bit and sauntered over to the shop.

There were two young girls manning the snack area of the drug store. One was tall and somewhat voluptuous, had perhaps been around the block a time or two, and chatted up the handsome young man at the counter. But my dad's attention was riveted immediately on the tiny brunette, perhaps fifteen years old, quiet and calm. He watched her as the older girl took his order — chocolate malt. "Thin," my dad added. "I like to drink it, not spoon it." The shorter girl glanced his way and began to make the shake. Dad waited, observing, and then picked up the frosty glass in his large hand and sipped. It was perfect, just the way he liked it.

And so it began. The courting went on as the two continued with high school, although my dad dropped out his last semester and was subsequently drafted into the Army. He didn't do well there, as he was transferred a bit of a distance from home and was terribly homesick. He lost weight. Looking at pictures from that time, it is easy to tell when he was just enlisted, contrasted with when he was serving. We found dozens of love letters from the two during that time. Dad repeatedly says how undeserving he is of Mom's love, and what a wastrel he was. The lack of self-esteem rang loud and clear in those sad letters.

My parents had a horrendous time, emotionally, while my father was in the service. In August of the year my mother was seventeen, against the wishes of her mother, these two lovey doves took off for Yuma (a frightening thought in the times before air conditioning) and eloped. As a Catholic, then, my mother would have been living in sin in an unblessed marriage. Her mom was very upset at the whole arrangement. Dad's parents were more accepting, and permitted the two to live in their already crowded two-bedroom home in Santa Ana. To his credit, my father began studying the religion, and joined the church. Eventually my grandmother melted in view of the clear and ever-present passion my parents were consumed by. By then, dad was also out of the Army, having been given a release from duty.

It was a different time. With the Great Depression and the second major world war, some people reacted by acting on their passions, living for today. They accepted a windfall and shared it with family or friends, enjoying it immediately. Others became more careful, saving, waiting, keeping to themselves. My parents were of the first type, and remained that way throughout their lives. Because their income was always fairly basic, they learned to live just barely within it, rarely able to defer, to save, to plan for the future. Some of their peers, generally those who had experienced poverty as well, lived their lives in a similar fashion. As part of a set of seminars held at my school district, a presentation on Generational Poverty was given. For me, it explained a great deal about my parents' life philosophies and spending habits.

But no one could deny that my parents were meant for one another. Their passion and affection for one another never faded. They held hands under the table, kissed when passing in the hallway, and cuddled in bed until Mom passed away. For sixty-three years they looked forward to seeing each other after work, spent every free moment together, and rarely fought. After my mother died, my father spent ten months just waiting for the chance to be with her again. He stated that it was only his religious beliefs of suicide preventing his going to heaven which kept him alive.

In Chicago, just before those California events began, my husband's parents met in a manner many young couples do — through siblings. Jean had plenty of them to provide fodder for dating experiences. With her five sisters and a fairly short spread of years among them, she saw loads of eligible young bachelors traipsing through the family's front door. Many of them might have held her interest, but one in particular had a great interest in her.

Howard had dated Jean's just-older sister, Faye. In the course of picking Faye up for an evening, he had caught sight of the younger girl. Right away he knew that this might be the preferred sibling for him. Jean returned the attentions.

Although Jean's family was large, it had generally been prosperous. Her father worked for Hormel, so there was always meat on the table. Thrifty and resourceful, her parents raised the six girls to be the same — all of them were taught to cook, clean, sew; many of them had artistic or other creative abilities which were explored with the limited additional resources on hand. Howard was attending the University of Chicago, and was a very bright and capable science student. He had caught the eye of Enrico Fermi, and began to work under him under the pre-Manhattan project.

After a respectful courtship time, the two were married and soon moved to Oak Ridge, Tennessee for the Manhattan Project. There, my husband was born. Howard then moved the family to Los Alamos, New Mexico to work for the Atomic Energy Commission. Into the fifties, Howard's skills in atomic energy and related engineering fields led him to California to work in private industry. The family prospered without Jean ever having to work a day. On Howard's salary they bought nice homes, saved, sent the kids to college, and fared well. Howard's eye was always on the future and the economy. He read and listened to a variety of information sources on which to base his financial decisions.

These two families of the Depression fared so differently for a number of reasons, but a key one was education. And another determining factor was the upbringing and economic level of the parents and grandparents. In all cases, how well they fared appeared to be nearly predetermined.

But one thing both the Liles and the Parsons had in common was a commitment to succeed as a loving family. And, in both cases, they accomplished that goal, passing on that model to their children. My brother and I, and Jeff's brother and he himself all had long-term marriages with children who are carrying on that tradition — of selecting and keeping a life partner, of nurturing and growing that relationship. We certainly have our ancestors to thank for providing us with shining examples of how to commit.

This is not to say that those marriages were perfect. My own parents had some enabler tendencies, certainly in terms of spending, in not delaying gratification. It is interesting to note that my brother and his wife did not follow that part of the model; they were excellent providers, gave their son a parochial school education and helped him obtain his Bachelor's, Master's degrees and a PhD in Sociology. They assisted Joe and his wife and young daughter in myriad ways, both financially and by physical support in terms of babysitting at the drop of a hat so that Joe and his wife could finish their education. To this day Bill and Gloria are frugal and predominantly non-materialistic. They take care of their possessions and donate generously of their time and talents to their church and community. And their value of history and tradition is deep.

Jean and Howard bickered a great deal. This bothered me a lot, and there were times when the tension was thick and caused me some stress. We were around them frequently, at least one day a week. Few conversations with Jean were not peppered with criticism of Howard. And yet she seemed adamant about maintaining the status quo. She rarely aimed the complaints to the right person.

But now, with Jean's dementia, Howard has moved into the caregiver mode, and he is resolute about keeping things as they are as long as possible. Moving Jean into an assisted living facility is something he won't consider as an option. His devotion to her, also tempered with a desire not to run out of money, keeps him tied to her even in her deteriorating state.

Both of our sets of parents have been victims of the planned obsolescence of the teetering retirement system. Social security and pensions have been unable to keep up with the rising survival ages. Jean and Howard are 90. It seems to be the case that one has to obtain a reverse mortgage on one's home by 80 to keep up with the costs of medical and pharmaceutical expenses.

It is my hope to pass both what we have earned and what we have learned on to our children and grandchildren, offering them a legacy we built. If all goes well, each of them will have a great set of assets passed down to them upon which they can build their own futures.

I also hope that they carry on with the tradition begun generations ago and continued by most of the members of the Liles and Parsons couples, which is to fully commit to a marriage and see it through until death takes one or both partners. It is heartbreaking for children to have to witness a marriage falling apart, and to long for whichever parent is absent. As an educator, I have witnessed firsthand the anguish experienced by children *who cannot focus on their studies due to their minds being occupied by strife in the home, or the loss of a parent. Choosing a life partner and sticking with that person through thick and thin seems to be falling out of vogue, as is the old custom of maintaining a relationship with a company. It is just too easy to move on. Roots are highly underrated. Looking back, I can see how well they served most of those who came before me, and I can only hope that my kids build those same kinds of solid connections and truly experience the deepening love of a decades-long romance.*

The phone tree out on the block wall that curves around the entrance of USC University Hospital begins with me, branches out to my generation, then off to those both older and younger. Thus, I don't have as much contact with my parents or parents-in-law, leaving it up to my brother to pass news on to our parents, and my sister-in-law to inform the Parsons side how Jeff is doing. It is hard not to speak with everyone directly, but after awhile it seems as though all I do is repeat myself, and I don't always recall if I fill everyone in equally. The story always alters a bit with the repeated telling.

My father never told me much about his childhood family life. Oh, there were plenty of stories about his activities in depression-era East St. Louis, Illinois. I heard about the doughnut-eating contests among his cohorts and the corkball games in the street. His vivid descriptions of the dusty neighborhood, tricks played on oldsters and the self-deprecating put-downs came frequently and easily, especially towards the end of his life. Even in poverty, Dad and his young brothers had a bounty of adventures from which they often emerged relatively unscathed. A few details of his short military service during World War II were hastily replaced by his first encounter with my mother, how she prepared milkshakes to his ideal (thin) at the soda fountain, and how gorgeous she was, how entirely smitten he was.

But I heard about his father and his first stepfather from others — Dad's mom, or Aunt Maude, who married the middle boy. Others told me of the first divorce, precipitated by a physical struggle with my dad as the literal rope in a desperate tug-of-war. Uncles recalled bits of information about the second relationship, its mirror to the first. Third time was the charm: a real grandpa for Bill and me and my cousins, a real dad for those, by that time, three boys.

My father always regarded women as superior beings, to be revered and treasured, if not completely understood. After all, we can't truly comprehend perfection, we mortal souls, can we? His discovery of my mom, the sweet, beautiful, nearly flawless creature, provided me, much later, with the revelation of Dad's prism, his idyllic vision of women. His one complaint about my mom, in their failing years, was that she would not allow him to wait on her as he felt she deserved to be. Her death left him even more bereft that I had thought he would be. His darling one, his anchor, his soul, had vanished. His own death, on what would have been their sixty-fourth anniversary, was a blessing.

I never heard my dad talk about his parents, his multiple fathers, because it could have been construed as a criticism of his mother's choices. All he would provide was polish and luster. Any tarnishing of her image, or of my mom's, would have to come from others.

The other day my brother forwarded me some scanned photos sent to him by our newly-found cousin, Larry. This man had stumbled upon our father's obituary while working on his ancestry data and had dug up information on us, his long-lost relatives. In the course of conversations with Larry, Bill has discovered and shared a treasure box of information on people we never even knew existed.

My father's mom had a storied life. A wing-walker and motorcycle racer, she latched onto our grandfather, Thomas, and escaped what she had felt was a mundane, dead-end life in Missouri. Barely out of her teens, she wanted to continue her wild life, and Thomas was just the man to show it to her. Unfortunately, by the time my father came along, the relationship had deteriorated in a dramatic fashion. At age ten, dad visited his grandmother for the first time, meeting up with some half brothers and sisters. But loyalty to his mom caused him to reject all other advances from the east coast contingency of his family. Until Larry's serendipitous finding, there was no further contact with the Liles clan.

Despite my grandfather's early bouts with lack of anger management, he apparently managed to go on to lead a fairly normal life with another woman, and maintained good connections with the rest of his family. The photos sent on to my brother and me show content individuals, frozen lifetimes ago. But those who remain, the descendents of my grandfather and his kin, are compassionate, welcoming folk. They trace their lineage to the first families of Tennessee, and have a rich and varied history that nurtures them to this day — and, now, it pulls Bill and me into its embrace. Truly, there are at least two sides to every story.

It is not often the case that Jeff's and my family's two sides get together. None of us has a dining area big enough for all of us to fit, now that a new generation of cousins exists. So it is interesting, in the waiting room, to see them interacting. It's a damned shame it takes something of this magnitude to bring all sides into the same building, because they all get along so well. From different backgrounds, disparate levels and types of education, common ground is instantly found.

Growing up, I had seen the men in my life working with tools. The women did not. Up and down the street men would do yard work and hammer various objects in the evenings and on the weekends. My dad could do some simple car repairs and build a workbench. Mostly, his talents lay in the garden. His job was at Armstrong Nurseries, doing some landscape design on the side, but mostly selling and delivering plants and trees and offering advice on how not to kill them. He was very good at what he did; he knew the Latin names of things and the relationships of the phyla of the plant kingdom. Most of this he learned on his own, by reading and paying attention, by having an innate ability to categorize, see similarities and differences and understand the underpinnings of botany. His designs looked completely professional and were hand-drawn in a very precise and exacting fashion on drafting paper using stencils. His execution was just as defined. He had the artist's eye for balance, filling spaces three-dimensionally with variations in plant height, going for textures and reserving some white space.

After he died, Shauna and I found three or four sketches he had done, mostly landscapes. A more confident man would have pursued and developed that talent. Yet, a more confident man would have gone much farther in any field. Dad was certain that he was shallow and pretty much worthless. He never understood what Mom saw in him. Rarely have I run across anyone with less self-esteem than my father, and few would be more deserving of an ego.

Dad was curious about things. Without much of a higher education — he got his GED more than twenty years after high school, then took some coursework at the community college — he could hold his own in a conversation. With his deep, melodious voice, frequent smile and self-deprecating humor, he was a personable man that many warmed to quite quickly. There was so much more to him than he ever gave himself credit for.

Animals understood that Dad was infinitely approachable. We always had dogs as I was growing up, and often had parakeets, some with a huge amount of personality for creatures so small — a personality Dad would bring out with lots of attention and affection. With his outdoor work, he had occasion to live among birds. His whistling mimicked their songs, and was of the quality of the work heard in "The High and the Mighty" — perfectly on-key, with a wide range, vibrato and change in volume. He often whistled as he did mundane chores. As a result, he was one of those rare folks that birds felt at home coming close to, buzzing around him or even landing on his finger, head or shoulder. It was something to see a man with his strong build whispering softly and grinning widely as a hummingbird perched on his hand. With animals, he didn't have to put on a mask and could be exactly who he was.

Dad was first and foremost a family man. He absolutely adored my mother and viewed her as a perfection she never could have been. He never went out with friends, although one would visit our home from time to time for a game of chess. Bowling once a week was a diversion, but my mom went, too, and sometimes they were able to play on the same team. I don't recall my parents going out together for date nights, since we couldn't afford that luxury. So all of the time they weren't at work they were with my brother and me.

As artistic and musical as he was, Dad definitely was methodical. He required symmetry. After a formal family dinner, when the dining table had been opened and lengthened with a leaf, he would take on the responsibility of making sure that it was repositioned exactly under the chandelier, and that each chair took its spot the same distance away from the table as the others. The tablecloth or doily would be centered exactly in the middle of the table. When conversing at the table he would arrange and rearrange utensils and napkins nearby, or quietly tap out a rhythm on his jumpy leg. There was always movement.

The need for everything in its place was reflected in his garage as well. Never have I seen such an orderly workspace as my father's garage. All tools were wiped and replaced after use, cords re-coiled neatly, everything re-boxed until the original boxes fell apart. Items were placed in spaced rows and kept with logical order. Decorations for holidays were kept in the same fashion and, afterwards, everything was put away exactly as it had been stored previously. In the house, the kitchen was kept the same way; dishes and small appliances were always cleaned and put back immediately after use. The same was true for the bathroom. So there was a respect for tools and other implements throughout the house. This is how I was raised.

Then I met Jeff. Then I met Jeff's family. I was still in college, around 19 years old, and it was a time of upheaval and experimentation – 1970. The Parsons made my parents' political and social views seem very conservative, by comparison. There was some order at their house, but a far larger quantity of everything, which lent itself to organized clutter. Stacks of magazines and piles of newspapers awaited decisions on their fate. The garage was stuffed with more tools than my father could ever have gathered, nor would he have felt the need for them (or even known their function). Also, there were precision instruments and many power tools. Howard and his boys could create and repair ANYTHING, and did so with abandon. A rebuilt Mustang which had, when they got it, the back end pushed into the back seat, stood operational in the driveway. The back end of the house, a pond, shelving, and hanging artwork testified to the acceptance of creativity and confidence in all members of that household. Yet there was no bragging, no flaunting of ego. They were what they were, what you saw was what you got – a man who had worked with Fermi during WWII and was now a senior scientist for Hughes, his wife, the artist and homemaker, and two boys who were not afraid to work on anything, try anything, followed by a creative and expressive daughter. The Parsons household was far afield from the one I had been raised in. But my future husband held many similarities to my dad, which unfolded over the years.

Like my dad, Jeff enjoyed spending time around his family, but not necessarily WITH *them. He wanted me home, but might not be in the same room with me for the whole of an evening. Similar to our dogs, Jeff was happiest when the pack was together, but didn't need all members of it to be within view or shouting distance.*

Jeff loved dogs but could have lived without cats. Part of this was because he was allergic to them, but he also didn't get their independent personalities. He liked dogs because of their love for play and affection and the need they had for people to take care of them. He also had an affinity for plants. For the delicate ones, he designed and built a fully functional greenhouse in our backyard with a heater which ran on a thermostat, mist irrigation system, and automatic bump-out roof panels for the fans to keep everything cool. The hardier ones lived in the yard. From time to time we had a vegetable garden, which had to make way for the expanding house. Jeff also really dug tools but didn't have the level of reverence my dad did for them. Tools were implements to get Jeff something else that he wanted or perceived that he/we needed, a means to complete a project. In and of themselves they had less value, so they weren't accorded the same treatment they would have gotten in my dad's garage. In fact, they littered the workbenches, floor, all flat surfaces. They were never kept in meaningful groups. Often they meandered into the house or out to the backyard, only to languish until tripped over, perhaps even longer than that. For Jeff, tools were a means to an end. For my dad, they were an end in and of themselves.

Also, Jeff's intuitive understanding of how tools work led him to his depth of knowledge on how machines worked. He could be shown a piece of equipment which was faulty, needing repair, or which was incomplete. So perfect was his grasp of mechanics that he could figure out its function, fix the thing and get it going again. I could recall each time we had a repair person out to our home, because it happened so rarely. Jeff did all the appliance and vehicle maintenance and repair work. He designed and built a two-story two-room family room over the course of three and a half years that doubled the size of our house and became the heart of it. The weekend our second child was born he went into helping with labor and delivery after having finished the rebuild of the 1960 Chevy truck my parents had sold/ given to us. He also rebuilt a 1960 TR3-A roadster, the Mustang from his family, and worked on all the other cars we owned, regardless of make or model.

Having seen his mother and grandmother sewing quilts and clothing as he was growing up, and understanding the machine which was involved, he commandeered our new sewing machine as soon as we bought it. While I made dresses, Halloween costumes and pajamas for our girls from patterns, he bought kits from mail order companies and made down-filled parkas and sleeping bags, tents, backpacks, and let me help with the snow outfits for the kids. Then he created a down comforter for our bed, since I was always so cold in the winter (In Southern California? Give me a break!). One of the projects he wanted to try out was upholstery for the car. I'm sure it would have turned out beautifully.

Furniture making was not out of the realm of his talents, either. Beginning with kits, he assembled a grandfather clock, some wall clocks and an icebox. Eventually he moved on to designing his own creations, such as an apple press for making cider and other juices to be fermented into wine and a beautiful breakfront with hutch that stood at the top of the stairs. His brother designed and mounted the three doors on the bottom of that later, perfectly matching the detailing and stain. My husband also made a hammered dulcimer for me on Christmas and a music stand for it. It remains to be properly tuned. And I haven't learned anything about playing it, either, but enjoy listening to others doing that on some CDs I've collected.

Of course, all of these efforts require their own special tools. The collection in the garage seemed to grow exponentially with each additional project. The number of tools good for only one specialty and the reluctance on the part of my husband to part with ANY of them made it so the fact that he had increased the size of the two-car garage by nearly fifty percent during the family room addition was negligible. The quantity of objects and, on occasion, their size, could be augmented by additional space. And the white space in that garage shrank with each passing year. Of course, Jeff rented a storage space across town which he filled with some truly worthless objects and boxes and boxes of magazines. But the air got rarer and rarer at our home.

The other aspect of my dad which resonated in Jeff was lack of confidence. In my husband, this manifested itself in ways my dad's did not. Jeff had issues performing in an academic setting. I believe he might have been afflicted with dyslexia, insofar as his writing and some math topics were concerned. Jeff seemed to hit the wall, so to speak, with some subjects. Grammar and spelling rules were completely random so far as he knew, and handwriting and printing were conventions he never came close to mastering. In fact, a lack of small motor coordination might have been part of the problem. His mastery of the verbal and of semantics reflected his far-ranging reading. But encoding the written word was painful for him. Because of these trials, his grades in school and later in college did not demonstrate his intelligence. Two of his children show some signs of these issues; his second daughter with math, spelling and grammar, and his son with study skills.

Jeff also felt quite ill at ease in social situations until he had a few sips of beer or wine in him. Given a glass or two he could be as loquacious and glib as the best of them. But he never seemed to feel socially adequate until alcohol leveled the playing field for him. Then he would smile widely, laugh often and lean forward, engaged fully in a conversation. I loved seeing him let go around others and wondered if I were to tape him, if he would see how easy being with others could be for him. I noticed his new job at Thermo Electron as a customer service engineer, where he had to go to different labs each day and interact often with strangers, seemed to help him loosen up a bit. But it was still an effort for Jeff to use interpersonal skills.

While it was true that my dad enjoyed both watching sports on TV and playing a few *of them, such as corkball when he was young and, later bowling and golf, Jeff liked more non-traditional, individual sporting activities. Jeff was a hiker and camper, and dabbled in fishing, mountain climbing and cross-country skiing. Once in awhile he would watch a few Olympic events with me, but preferred the history channel or PBS. But he was never the type to spend weekends in front of the TV observing football or baseball. The only time those would appear on our set would be when my dad visited.*

If it is true that those of us who have good familial relationships seek out our parents' personality traits in our future partners, then I think I can add myself to those ranks. The parts of my dad that were his best aspects and his perceived flaws, I found in Jeff. He was no neat freak, but his love of growing things, desire to improve his surroundings and his mind, and, yes, his self-doubts, were all my dad's traits, too. Plus, both of them had great hair and beautiful, expressive, light green eyes. ;)

I wonder if I reminded Jeff of his mother. Lately it is harder to discern similarities.

Twice a year I head down to California to visit old colleagues, neighbors and relatives. The focus of those visits is usually Jean and Howard, Jeff's parents, who are no longer physically able to travel up to visit me. Today I am in Southern California; this afternoon I will be driving over to their house, bringing lunch, and picking their brains for this book.

Howard is still a very sharp man. At nearly ninety, he maintains a very busy lifestyle, enlisting the help of willing neighbors to do improvements on the inside and outside of their house, working on a model railroad layout recreating the Chicago shipyards in the long upstairs attic, and watching out for Jean, who has Alzheimer's and some movement issues involving her hips and knees. Occasionally moving her arms around is also quite difficult. Movement is getting much more difficult for Howard as well. He shuffles more than walks and leans heavily on furniture he passes. His breath is wheezy as he exerts himself. But the mind is still entirely there, and he converses freely.

It seems so very long ago that Howard helped Jeff build the double family room onto our home in Chino. Howard designed not only the staircase for the Chino house, but also the roof for the family room. Anything involving places where non-right angle edges came together, Howard was the go-to guy. Howard used training from a class he took at Wilson Junior College in Chicago in 1940, called Descriptive Geometry, and the problems he described having solved there were very much in line with those architects and builders would encounter on the job. Anything tricky involved with our home improvements would require Howard's stamp of approval.

The main topic of conversation when I was there the other day was their dog, Gigi. She is a tiny overweight manic white poodle whom they both adore. She makes every effort to run the household; their leadership seems to be getting more tenuous with each visit I make.

I was a nervous wreck the first time I came to call on Jean and Howard. I can't recall how long Jeff and I had been together at that point, but together enough, I suppose, for him to take me home to meet his parents. Once we got to his house, he rather left me on my own. I recall burbling out at some point, "So how is everyone in this wonderful house this beautiful day?" to dead silence. Polite, yet dead just the same. It remains one of the most embarrassing moments of my life, and yet as I recall it I am smiling ruefully. It's not as though they kicked me out for abject silliness at that moment.

The house that I found so amazing thirty-eight years ago is aging. Howard has led the charge on cleaning up and refurbishing in and out, but the daily grime shows. He has macular degeneration, finds it hard to read print on the computer or on paper, and simply doesn't see a lot of the dirt and bits of food which seem to be everywhere. I know the neighbors come over frequently, since they are working on the projects Howard outlines for them, but I wonder if they are allowed to do cleaning — that was always Jean's domain, and it is hard for her to give it up, yet she does none of it anymore.

I had noticed the last few times I've been with Jean that she is bathing very infrequently, washing her clothing less, and has quite a growth of whiskers on her upper neck and chin. With Howard's reduced vision and Jean's desire not to be messed with, this isn't likely to get better. I recall having several arguments with my father about cleanliness, too. I am assuming that this is yet another by-product of Alzheimer's.

Two days ago when I visited them right after touching down at the airport, I stayed for a couple of hours, leaving in plenty of time to get back to Brad and Donna's before dark. During conversations, I noticed Jean chiming in far less than she had in the past. In phone talks with the couple, mostly Jean would respond with rinse-and-repeat types of general statements, and come up with the same topics, usually about the neighbors, the dog, or Madison, over and over, and often have issues with word retrieval, all things I had observed with my dad. I am glad to see that she is still reading, at least, but the quiet I saw this week was troubling.

I see many of the same tell-tale signs of their needing more help each time I am here. From some of the stories I have heard about Jean's dementia, I have to think it won't be long before a caregiver or assisted living is required. The situation is quite similar to that of my parents the year or so before Mom passed away. I did tell Howard about some of the services my folks had taken advantage of through SCAN, the county Medicare supplement program, and he has opted to choose from the menu of services provided, but mainly only the meal options. I plan to remind him sometime during this trip about the cleaning and meal preparation that is also available for extremely reasonable costs.

Jeff was very close to his parents and siblings. Having no real close friends, just acquaintances at work and in the neighborhood, his ties to his family remained the strongest. So those were the folks with whom he socialized, the people we spent our weekends and holidays with (my parents had Christmas Eve and birthdays, but the remainder of special events were Parsons-oriented). So my bonds with my in-laws remain rather strong, compared to those I have heard about in other families. Howard was the one who lent us money for the down payment on the only house we bought together, the one in Chino; Jean was the one I called nearly every day about child-rearing when Shauna was tiny. In the early years of our marriage, we went to their home just about every Saturday evening for homemade pizza or take-out cannelloni. The girl, or girls, dependent on the era, and Jean and I would always take a walk around the block, strolling slowly to make sure the kids had time to sniff a flower, explore the path a bug was taking, or talk for a bit with a neighbor. A bit later on, after we had bought the house, Sunday dinners were on us — usually a baked chicken, a roast, or a stew. But, in any case, a weekly visit was de rigeur.

When the girls were tiny, they had the same routine with their grandfather. When Howard would walk in, Toddler Shauna would declare, "Weed a book!" and take him by the hand, leading him over to the couch. Jeremie, at the same age, would assert, "GO!", pulling him over to the door for a brief stroll up and down the sidewalk.

I vacillate between longing to be alone and treasuring each visit from family members. While it can be relaxing to just zone out for the time periods when Shauna and I are kicked out of Jeff's hospital room, I never get away from where we are anchored. But when Parsons or Liles folks come to offer support, they not only bolster me up, but also provide a welcome distraction from the sterile walls and corridors of this facility. After a few minutes of being caught up in the activities going on outside these walls, it becomes easy to get swept along in conversation peppered with humor and warmth.

In both the Parsons and the Liles families, normal, everyday dialog was anything but. Growing up, I was exposed to and participated in a great deal of teasing and storytelling. Joking around was the norm. If you didn't have a sense of humor, you wouldn't have survived long in that family.

The males specialized in funny voices. Dad, especially, enjoyed lowering his voice and adopting strange accents and syntax from unknown realms. One that he used often resembled Yiddish, but wasn't quite there. His favorite alternate name was Irving Schmidlap.

This was during the heyday of the variety show, a TV staple for a generation. Carol Burnett, Ed Sullivan, Dean Martin and a group of other crooners, the Smothers Brothers and the late-night hosts all ran with skits and monologues and were rife with one-liners. We watched them all; well, the kids had to go to bed early, but we participated as much as we were allowed to. Anything for a laugh, at our house. Emulating his would-be mentor, Victor Borge, Dad would launch into what sounded like a straight-up song and turn it into a parody. And, like Borge, there was a lot of talent there that got covered up with the self-deprecating humor.

Saturday morning cartoons provided a whole other schtick for my family. We watched only the Warner Brothers types, since my dad shunned the Hanna Barbera variety. Elmer Fudd and Bugs Bunny performing opera was the highlight of any possible cartoon show. ("Kill the Wabbit, kill the wabbit, kill the wabbit!" sung to Flight of the Valkyries and the whole barber shop bit to Figaro were standouts.) Saturday nights at bedtime seemed to be the occasion for my father's monster intoning and groaning, accompanied by a darkened hallway and a flashlight shining beneath his chin. Of course, there was also the de rigueur Frankenstein stroll. Then he would remark to my mom that he couldn't understand why his kids couldn't get to sleep. Naturally, this followed an afternoon of vampire and alien black and white flicks on the local channels and Elvira in the evening. My brother is an official Elvira Fan Club member to this day. And I have a hard time getting to sleep without having my covers just over my ears to avoid both vampire bites and that Aliens From Mars kinda needle in the back of your neck that turned you into a Martian Slave thing. Fifty years later. Lots of education later. Lots of common sense and parenting. All for nothing.

My brother liked to emulate masters-of-ceremonies with his fist under his chin resembling a mic. His eyebrows would join his hairline and he would lean in as though he were conducting an interview. Imitating his favorite deejay, Wolfman Jack, was another pastime of his. With both my dad and my brother, taking on alternative personas when just having a regular conversation around the table was the norm.

With my mom and her mom, Nanny, it wasn't about getting into someone else's skin just to talk. But both of them were teasers and loved to laugh. They got their jollies in a more normative fashion, telling stories about their upbringing on farms and silly family tales. A *lot of teasing went on when anyone in the house had a failure of any type. For Nanny, since she did a lot of the cooking and baking the years she lived with us — between husbands — any failing in the kitchen merited merciless teasing for years after. And, of course, we kids provided plenty of fodder to be taunted about, as well.*

So getting serious at the Liles home was rare and actually kind of scary. For the most part, it involved a discussion of politics or social norms, and my dad and I disagreed on many key points, such as religion, abortion, and sometimes, but less often, politics. As I entered college, I was exposed to viewpoints I hadn't grown up with, and some of them made more sense to me. Of course, I brought them home for hashing out with my parents, with varying success. My folks were pretty much hard line Democrats, but I was leaning towards Peace and Freedom at that point. The Vietnam War was going on, and my brother was in the Army, stationed in Germany. Things began to get dicey between my father and me. I recall one emotional afternoon as I approached the house, coming home from work. Dad and I had had a very heated social issues argument the night before. I walked up the driveway and noticed him standing in the open garage. Giving him a cursory greeting, I headed for the door, but he stopped me with a question. "How can we stop doing this to each other?" He was clearly upset. At that point, to keep the peace, we had to agree to have certain hot topics forbidden. If a conversation got around to an issue we knew we had very disparate points of view on, we would just veer off to another type of conversation altogether. We agreed to disagree, because we loved one another too much to feel that awful around each other, dreading the next cause we could never hope to resolve to bubble to the surface.

Another couple of clowns in my family were my uncles, Dad's brothers. Dad was the oldest boy, followed by Bobby and then David, both sons of Dad's stepdad, Bob Winning. Bobby was a very self-effacing, down to earth kind of guy. He loved telling stories about their childhood, remembering characters from their neighborhoods who went over the line to get what they wanted. Often these characters were relatives. Like my father, Bobby was not the stereotypical blue collar worker; both were thoughtful, noticed details and had an artistic bent. This talent was taken even farther with their brother, David. While my dad did a handful of sketches, then got discouraged because of the time it was taking to make things look exactly as they did in his head, David had fewer compunctions about that, and was more willing to see art as fluid and changeable. Dave was also a prankster. He loved playing tricks on us youngsters, so he made a fabulous babysitter the few times my parents entrusted him with that job. I recall one very hot summer in Lakewood that Bill and I complained that we were burning up. Dave put us in a cool bathtub. I continued to whine that the water was coming out of the tap too warm to really cool us off, and remember shrieking in delight when Dave's response was to empty a tray of ice cubes into the tub.

So I took all this joking around with me in my new relationship, noticing that the Parsons liked to mess around as well. However, the tenor of the teasing and verbal horseplay was somewhat different. It was almost a class difference, or perhaps small town versus urban humor. My parents were from poorer backgrounds with more of a small-town or rural feel. The Parsons were from Chicago, and had college under their belts. It was interesting that visual slapstick was a popular form of humor in the Parsons male enclave, at least in what they chose to watch on TV. Then there was the British humor component, a la Monty Python and Benny Hill – the ribald, topless innuendo that could pass on British TV but not American, at least not in prime time. After Jeff and I were married, Saturday evenings were often spent at his parents' on the couch watching the popular sitcoms of the day – Mary Tyler Moore, All in the Family and the like. We were The Meathead to the world's Archie Bunker.

The Monty Python skits and one-liners were thrown around the house in infinite combinations and situations. But it was not about the sound of the voice, as it had been when I was growing up – the emphasis was on the words and their meaning.

Mirroring my Uncle Bobby's storytelling skills, Howard, given a glass of wine at a family gathering, would launch into an explanation with some scientific or historical validity – at least it would sound that way. He would cite references and sound perfectly authoritative. Then, when a critical point in the story had been reached and one of us would ask a leading question or flat-out call Howard out, he would tell us in a deapan voice that he had made it all up. I never saw it coming. His wife, Jean, would use family quotes at offbeat moments. For example, Howard's mother, Molly, had two family-famous lines – "Nice to be busy!" and "Best years of your life..." usually stated when all hell was breaking lose in the household. Jean took those statements up and threw them around with abandon. A few of her own mother's memorable quotes were dredged up from time to time. With six daughters, her mom was often heard to exclaim, "Children, children, you are driving me to distraction!" at which point the kids needed to scatter. But my favorite Jean uttering was stated after some family member had ignored her sage advice. With a wry look she would claim her ultimate rule over the gathering with, "One word from me...and he does as he pleases."

So it was Liles funny voices, Parsons throw-away lines. No wonder my children are a mess.

However, it IS fun from time to time to see how the next generation has melded and altered these family jewels. My brother's son, Josef, is a complete master of impersonation. My own kids have taken sarcasm to an art form. And Brad's two offspring have memorized sizable tracts from musicals, comedic movies and plays, performing them with proper accents in place, timing perfect – you might as well be playing a YouTube track.

Finally, there are puns. Groaners. Milk-spurting episodes where you say just the right thing at the wrong moment. This can get quite competitive, one building upon the former until people just have to leave the room.

So having a sense of humor is required in the Liles-Parsons fusion family. If you don't have much of one at the outset of your visit among us, either you'll have gained an appreciation for it or lost the will to live.

The Seventh Night

I was unable to get to a computer but managed to get outside the hospital to place phone calls whenever there was a shift change, so I called one of the admins of my website and asked her to post this:

Update from Sue:

I talked to Sue briefly this afternoon. Jeff had surgery yesterday, and it was successful. However, he is still on a respirator to assist with his breathing, and is expected to be in the hospital for at least another 12 days (mostly in ICU). But he is making progress, and right now the prognosis is good. I'll up date further as I hear from Sue. As you can imagine, she is quite exhausted.

Please keep Jeff and Sue both in your thoughts.

Shauna and I settle into a routine at the second hospital. The staff here is much more welcoming and compassionate, which is reflected in their relaxed rules. Arrowhead neurologists were certain that the frequent and prolonged presence of friends and loved one was detrimental to the recovery of stroke victims. This is not the philosophy at USC. Here we are given a cardio chair, semi-reclined, along with warmed blankets to help us get some rest at night. Each night one of us is in that chair in Jeff's room, sharing space with myriad machines and their accompanying wires and cables. The other is in the waiting room reading or trying to sleep.

It is a different life here. At home, my day is ruled by lists and calendars. Here there is only the ebb and flow of the hospital routine, and every day there is new information and new test results and interruptions of that routine. I have to relinquish all control over this situation and learn to adapt.

The prompt on the NaNoWriMo site, dedicated to getting people to concentrate on writing a novel for the month of November, read, "Why am I on your to-do list?" That one struck a chord with me.

Jeff and I are list makers. Most of mine are for the day, occasionally by the week, and I cross things out as I complete them, often thinking of something else to add. During holidays my lists can be very long, and once in awhile Jeff sees something on my list he feels he can help out with, which is a blessing.

Jeff has little yellow Unocal cardstock papers he brought home from work. They are just the right size to tuck into a pocket to bring along to Home Depot, and rarely get lost because of their distinctive size, rounded corners and color. On those he makes his chore lists and things to get at the hardware store or REI. I find these all over the garage and the house, as well as in the car, with his idiosyncratic printing, never maintaining a line, rarely containing proper spelling or grammar, and uniquely his own.

Once he glanced at one of my lists and discovered his name on there. At first he wondered if it was an incomplete thought – Jeff…iron his shirts? Jeff…tell him something? Jeff…buy him some deodorant?? When he finally gave up and asked me, and I just smiled cryptically and waggled an eyebrow, of course he figured it out. After that, I found he perused my subsequent lists with a great deal more interest than before.

One Christmas I bought a few peignoir sets and wrapped them up nicely for him. After he opened them, the kids had a hard time figuring that one out. However, they WERE really for HIM, weren't they?

One negligee pair in particular was a favorite of both of us. It was a statiny rich orange spaghetti strap teddy with a accompanying short robe. I adored the color and texture. At that point I was often spending the ends of my evenings in chat with my online Star Wars buddies, but on orange peignoir nights I knew I would need to sign off early, so I began to signal my friends by switching my font color ten minutes before I planned to go to bed. The orange italics font signal eventually took on a life of its own in our little online world, and was used by several of my friends to give us all TMI. But Jeff, you know, was on my list!

In the morning for shift change we dash out to make calls and grab something to eat in the cafeteria. After that we are back in the waiting room until we are allowed back in to be with Jeff. He is shuttled back and forth for tests or procedures. Several different specialists visit him in his room for respiratory therapy and other monitoring. The activity level here is much greater than at Arrowhead. I have the sense that the team here has a better handle on exactly how Jeff is doing. Dr. T, a neurologist, is the team lead. He has a deadpan demeanor and is all about flow charts, percentages and odds. His clinical attitude is at once reassuring, in that he is so authoritative, and depressing, since with each visit he seems to be giving us worse and worse news.

Nowadays I catch myself playing Spider Solitaire a great deal. After thousands of games, I've gotten pretty good at the highest level, winning nine percent of the games I play. I wonder how much of the attraction for me is less about how often I win and more about getting to UNDO moves that don't work well and RESTART games that aren't progressing as I'd like. This is a pastime that, given the same set of cards each time, but in different configurations, I can succeed at often enough to keep me coming back. Nine percent represents better odds for me than I have in other aspects of my life.

I learned this game from observing my husband. Catty-corner back to back, we would sit in the den in our swivel, colored fake leather desk chairs, each seated at our own computer at our own desk. I would be working on school preparations or grading, or, if finished with all that, checking out Star Wars fandom websites or chatting with fandom friends from all over the world online. He would be either doing work for his employer, a chemical laboratory equipment manufacturer, or playing Spider Solitaire. He liked the easy level, in part because he could be very successful at it, winning a large percentage of the games he attempted. Once in awhile he would work at some other online games that required puzzle solving or properly stacking or lining up objects. But Spider Solitaire was his default desktop entertainment. Only recently have I adopted his favorite game as my own.

I've never been a betting woman. You would never find me in Vegas or the local reservation casino. I tried it once, playing nickel slots in a smoky establishment down the road. After twenty dollars disappeared, I discovered this wasn't entertainment for me. For one thing, the choking cigarette haze that permeated the place was stifling. And the folks plugged into the machines had such low energy it was as though the whole place was on 'ludes. Plus, there went twenty bucks, for no fathomable reason. From what I have heard, the acts in the casinos aren't for me, either. Nothing about this scene is familiar, fun or comforting.

I wondered if Dr. T was a betting man. Constantly listing the odds, with each scenario getting bleaker and bleaker, he would be a bookie's nightmare. The flowcharts he verbally laid out for me, and that Jeff followed relentlessly down like a poorly-pitched pinball, the dominoes tipping one another over with heartless precision, all provided analogies one would think would have me swearing off games forever. "Never tell me the odds!" Han Solo growled in one of my favorite Star Wars scenes. What would Dr. T have done had I barked that at him? Would his expression even have changed? He didn't strike me as having much of a sense of humor.

I have an old friend, Ellie, a former colleague of mine from Chino Valley Unified. Her husband had a stroke shortly after mine did. Now I see her ghostly presence online almost every day, as yahoo informs me that she is joining yet another card-playing room between physical therapy sessions for her husband and the caregiving chores he requires. Canasta has become for her what Spider Solitaire is for me. The difference is, she can quit and join another game, but not really start over. There is no UNDO in Canasta.

Jeff never enjoyed board games. I would get him involved once in a great while, coaxing him to play with me and the kids, but he never got a kick out of it, so I stopped asking. Board games required a focus, a concentration I think he felt they didn't deserve. He would much rather watch a highly educational program or something completely silly (usually English comedies such as Fawlty Towers or Benny Hill) on TV or read a science fiction book — activities which he could do alone and abandon when they bored him. His ship and train models also provided that aspect — easy to take up another time if you felt like moving on to something else at the moment. Most of Jeff's free time was taken up by things he wouldn't have to sit still and finish right away.

I should talk. I preferred short stories to novels, small craft projects to long-term ones, chores I could finish up quickly as opposed to projects that dragged on for days and days. I wanted my instant gratification, and I wanted it now! On the other hand, I DID like things to be finished up quickly, or, at least, in a timely fashion. Jeff had no such compunctions. Leaving things lay for another day was perfectly fine with him. I had lists of chores which I ticked off with great satisfaction when completed; he made lists, ticked off a couple of items, then lost the list in a pile of unopened stuff from the hardware store, or left it in a shirt pocket to get run through the laundry and spread bits all around the dryer. I suppose, then, that that would give him a RESTART, wouldn't it?

What do miracles do to the kinds of odds doctors lay out for patients? Are they figured into all the statistics, or thrown out as anomalies? And, supposedly, praying can affect the outcome of even the worst, most hopeless case. What, then, of the odds? Are they only in effect when nothing metaphysical intervenes? When only the limitations of science and human anatomy decide the final prognosis? You always hear about patients fighting to survive. "He's such a fighter." Do fighters skew the aspects of probability involved in a terminal disease? Dr. T isn't indicating any options other than those he lists. He doesn't seem to take into account a man who enjoys life the way my husband does. But I could also see Jeff standing near the bed objectively taking in all the doctor is saying and totally buying into the scientific banter, completely getting the jargon, agreeing to follow the flow chart. He might question, but Dr. T's logic might get him, in the end.

Is Jeff a fighter? So far, I have been assuming that he would rally and we would get to go home, alter our lifestyles by adopting healthier eating and drinking habits, foregoing Solitaire for long walks and trips to Trader Joe's for organic produce and Twigs and Flakes. I would stay home as long as needed and help him with physical therapy. No more sixty-hour work weeks. No more beer brewing and wine making. No more me in the den chatting all evening with online people I have never even met. No more him in the family room alone watching Monty Python. I told him all this just the other day, when he was awake. We could kick this thing. He was only 58 years old. We still had a teenager at home to raise. Jeremie was expecting another grandchild for us in just a few weeks. We were going to retire in a couple of years and move up to Washington where Jeff could putter until the yaks came home, or head on down to the docks with a pile of ship model kits, wearing his watch cap, and lie to little kids all afternoon about his travels and adventures at sea. We planned to do day trips and hikes and spoil the grandkids. Jeff would get involved in the Scouting activities with the grandsons. We could still do a lot of that even if Jeff wound up not regaining use of his right side or ended up with a little slur in his speech, couldn't we?

UNDO UNDO UNDO UNDO

I realize I have no idea any longer about what is going on in the outside world, in Real Life. I have no internet connection, and conversations I have with people who are still living normal lives don't include a lot of current events. Jeff's and my everyday routine of the LA Times and the local paper at breakfast is on hold. The evening news isn't shown on the machines and monitors in his ICU room. Surely, we are living a fantasy here in the hospital.

Politically, one of the proudest moments I had as Jeff's wife was the day he came home shortly after our marriage and announced that he had stood up to someone in the Bastanchury Water Company office. I knew that was particularly hard for him, his being the new, young guy and all. But one of the salesmen had made a disparaging remark about Tom Bradley, an African-American who was running for mayor of Los Angeles. This comment had to do with Mr. Bradley's color. Jeff wheeled about, put a sneer on his face and remarked, "Wow. That's damned racist of you!" in a very sarcastic tone, from his reenactment later. Another person might have laughed along or said nothing. I loved that Jeff had the guts to speak up. By the way, Tom Bradley went on to serve for twenty years as mayor of one of the largest cities in the United States, and was the host mayor for the Olympics in 1984 — an event that many agreed was a hallmark of how-tos.

There were certainly a number of times when it felt hard to be so liberal in such a stiflingly conservative environment such as Orange County and, later, just across the hills from that in Chino. These areas were hotbeds, if they could be called that, of right-wing Christian values and politics, with large contingencies of Catholics and Mormons with their attending social stances. So, being agnostic extreme left-leaning tree-hugging granola-eating Sierra Club members with our attending socialist urges had us feeling left out and estranged from "the system". In college, I had marched for peace, protested the war in Vietnam, and walked fourteen miles for the first Earth Day. We used home and doctor's office childbirth and breastfed our babies. I voted Peace and Freedom. When Shauna was in junior high she came home and asked me how to protest their not having received the promised and funded concrete benches from the school district. I told her how to peacefully stage a sit-in during passing periods and lunch, how not to block doorways or interfere with the business of running the school. She wrote an editorial to the local paper and organized an orderly demonstration. The kids got their benches. Shauna also got kicked out of an eighth grade social studies class for questioning the views of the substitute teacher on how European nations should behave towards terrorists. I told her I was terribly proud of her. In high school and college, our girls brought home gay friends, whom we adored. Our oldest dated folks of color. Both girls, with our blessing, drove friends to Planned Parenthood for contraception. It was all good. But most of these were not values or concepts shared with neighbors, nor most colleagues.

At work there was a handful of liberals, but we were definitely in the minority. My neighbor, who was the school librarian where I worked, used to joke that she and her husband cancelled out my hubby and me at the polls. I must say that I was very proud of California voters recently when they elected "Moonbeam" Jerry Brown as governor and reinstated Barbara Boxer as US senator. The pendulum there is swinging back, too late for me to enjoy it firsthand, unfortunately.

Jeff and our son were also very involved in scouting. From first grade on, my husband helped as a parent leader first in Cub Scouts, then Boy Scouts. Jeff and I shared that responsibility for three years as den leaders, along with another gal. The boys met at our dining room table every Wednesday evening, as we methodically went through the scout manual and ran activities with the boys. We were lucky enough to have a great group of parents who assisted whenever we asked. Then there were the extra events and troop meetings to attend and supervise. Scouting took up a chunk of our lives; for the most part, we enjoyed our interactions with the kids and their parents.

The conundrum with being a liberal involved in boy scouting is, of course, the no-gay rule. It seemed to be the case in our troops (Cub Scouts and then Boy Scouts for fifth graders and up) that it just never came up – Don't Ask, Don't Tell for kids. And then there is the issue of boys needing to declare a faith in order to get their Eagle rank. Again, kids who weren't believers, like ours, just faked it. I am unsure how that affects kids, having, in both cases, to be someone they truly are not. It IS good to see some of those lovely young men now having the strength to come out; by the same token, it is absolutely unfortunate that they had to deny who they were and/or submerge their lack of religious fervor in order to gain all of the benefits scouting has to offer.

For my husband, being involved in boy scouting with his son allowed him to advance along with Jeff much further than he had gotten as a child. Certainly had he not been so into it, his son would have dropped out long before. In the end, Jeffy got his Eagle with a project that benefited my school – developing an emergency preparedness bin half a train car long. And his dad was able to proudly stand alongside him when he received the final badges and decorations.

For my part, I had helped with the PTA at my school in a variety of capacities for twenty-five years, as well as attending outings with my daughters in their Girl Scout troops through sixth grade. They both moved on to other activities after that, and we didn't push it. Softball, cheerleading, swim team and drama took the place of Girl Scouts. It's interesting that there seemed to be less of an emphasis on religion and sexuality in that organization.

In any case, the values my husband and I passed along to the kids consisted of non-spiritual, for the most part, yet long-lasting ideals. Jeremie recalls the emphasis on using yard space for growing things, and then following through with what you grew or gathered, such as canning, freezing, dehydrating or otherwise preserving those crops. What we didn't or couldn't grow, due to lack of space, we would go out and find. From Lodi the boys brought back fruit juice for winemaking, orchards in Beaumont and Banning out in the desert produced cherries, peaches, apples and nectarines for eating and jam and pie making, and a ranch there grew fresh turkeys for Thanksgiving and Christmas dinners. In the Fresno area, we found boysenberries to make jam and to freeze for pies in the winter. Picking most of the produce, and then racing home to process it was a family event. Neighbors and friends admired our skills and enjoyed a bit of the bounty for Christmas gifts.

Do it yourself tasks provided another skill set Jeff passed down. He was convinced that he could fix nearly any household object or vehicle; usually he was right. If he needed assistance, he would find a book and read up on it, or ask his father or brother for advice. The result was that we rarely needed to hire out. Also, when the kids would have car problems or an accident, Jeff would tell them where to get the parts and then tell them how to do the repair. Accidents, especially, provided two of our kids with more hands-on experience than they may have wanted to know about, certainly at that point in their lives. However, to this day they carry that spirit of trying things on their own.

Another gift their father gave them was a sense of thrift, of saving for a rainy day. If we needed an appliance or item of furniture for the house, Jeff would study and investigate which brand or source would be the best quality for the best price. Sometimes these considerations would go on for weeks; in the end, he would make the call, and then still worry about whether it was the optimum one. He was not a wasteful person, except possibly for the quantities of pasta he would purchase from Trader Joe's or Costco. We took care of what we had and milked it for as long as it could possibly last. Insofar as the savings went, Jeff began purchasing stock in kind from his first employer, continued that practice for years, and then made some strategic bond purchases. He built up a nice portfolio which enabled us to consider retiring before the age of 60. And all of the improvements he had made on the house had increased its value astronomically.

But perhaps the most important value we gave the kids was a sense of the importance of family. Both of us spent a great deal of time involved with the kids' activities, but we also devoted a lot of time to our parents. For Jeff, his family provided him with the friends he had few of. His brother and his father were probably the best friends he ever had, especially since they had so much in common: puttering, hobbies, building things, science, even British humor shows. Maybe because of that, Jeff never really felt the need to cultivate friendships outside of his family. Any socializing was with the Parsons. So the kids saw us choosing to spend spare time with family — with them, with their grandparents and extended family. All vacations were taken together as a family until the kids were so involved with college or jobs they couldn't attend. As a result, our children are family-oriented as well. That is a value I am glad to say we instilled in them.

Our daily routine – breakfast and the paper together, mentions of tasks for that day or meeting reminders, references to the calendar hanging on the front of the fridge, the gathering spot for information on what each of us was doing that month. When Jeff worked regular, predictable hours at Unocal, I would pack his lunch. Now, with his current job, we rarely know ahead of time what he'll be doing and in which lab until he calls in each morning. But the large calendar, originally intended as a desktop blotter, carries all of the other appointments, Jeffy's work schedule, and my school events. I keep a small dayplanner in my purse where I record my needed chores and job-related meetings held during school hours. PTA, birthdays, dentist appointments are all in there as well. I wonder when I will be able to get back home and begin to fulfill those obligations again, even the simple ones like the weekend household chores. I twist the ring on my left hand absently and see that a bit of the turquoise inlay is beginning to flake off.

The first piece of jewelry that Jeff ever gave me was for my birthday, shortly after we started to view ourselves as a couple. It was silver with a turquoise center, a kidney shaped stone. I had never seen anything like it. He had bought it on an excursion with his dad to Albuquerque, a town about which he had nothing good to say. In fact, he had sent me a postcard from there which read, "Greetings from Albuquerque which is really gross. It is Sunday and the sidewalks are all rolled up." But apparently he had found a shop which was open.

Jeff had spent part of his childhood in the Southwest. After working on the Manhattan Project in Oak Ridge, Tennessee, where Jeff was born, Jean and Howard had moved to Los Alamos, New Mexico — the secret city — and Howard went to work for the new Atomic Energy Commission. Although the very nature of that town caused the people there to develop a culture all their own, there was still plenty of the Southwest that leaked in. Many of the people found the Native American jewelry, décor, architecture, and culture charming and possessing a depth they found surprising. A good portion of the residents stayed on, in part because of the vast differences in lifestyle and customs which they assimilated into their own. Jeff's family had taken portions of those traditions with them when they moved to California.

For Jean, this made perfect sense. Not only did the Southwestern Native Americans of several different tribes present an artistic sense which was new to her and appealing to the artist within her, but in terms of fashion, the jewelry she found there was stunning and new. Squash blossom necklaces, needlepoint brooches, and silver feather earrings, as well as some decorative barrettes, set her apart when she wore them after they left the state. Later, as her hair began to turn a beautiful silvery gray, the colors of the native jewelry set it off elegantly.

One of the things that added to Jeff's mystery, I felt, was the fantastic clip watch he wore on his wrist. It was large, with ornate silverwork, and a type of large turquoise piece I had never seen before. The stones were from the Bisbee mine, and were considered very rare and valuable. In addition, I had never seen a watch that was held on to one's arm in that manner. With Jeff's large, muscular arms, the piece had the perfect setting.

So this ring was my introduction to Navajo jewelry. And it also provided a gateway to my understanding of the Parsons family.

Although all of their ancestors hailed from Europe, mainly Denmark and England, they were not averse picking up bits of other cultures they found in their travels. Again, with Jean's admiring eye and Howard's love of toys, plus both of their loves for history, their home reflected this eclectic and accepting attitude. So it was less of a strict adherence to a style of décor (my parents' choices) and more of a redefinition of style diversity and honoring the past and other traditions which prevailed in the Parsons household.

As we began to move past Early Donation and started being able to afford some pieces of our own choosing, some Southwest items joined our home. First off were our wedding rings, bought from the Disneyland Hotel, which had a fairly intense collection of Native American art. Matching, they were silver with inlay turquoise in a random pattern. They cost $28.00 apiece, and I paid for them as I was the one who was working at a paying job at the time. Jeff was working for his dad, trying to start up a new business called Scientific Instrument Services. We were unable to front the money for much in the way of art until after Jeffy was born, and at that point we started with blankets. On a Southwest vacation, we were at the trading post in Hubbell, Arizona late one afternoon, when suddenly the owner called out that everything was forty percent off for the next hour only. We scrambled to find just the right blanket before closing time, settling on a magnificent black, deep red, gray and off-white Storm design. It was small, perhaps measuring just under two feet by three feet, but the design was intricate, the colors true and the attention to detail unmatched. Jeff made a pressure clip out of wood and hung the rug in our new family room.

Having one really nice piece led to finding more. Jeremie found us another blanket, a Rainbow Ye'ii design, that was very old and had a couple of small stains, but the story it told was compelling. Shauna and Ward added to our collection by introducing some Northwestern pieces — a tiny bentwood box with orca patterns and a one foot high totem pole made by a young artist. Soon, each time we visited their area we added more to the Northwest contingency, yet each time Jeff traveled around the Southwest he brought me back a piece of jewelry or some small pots. Jeff was also a devotee of old tools, and found some interesting pieces which worked well with the Native American ones, especially as set off in that family room, with its extensive use of wood beams, paneling, and stone fireplace. A set of snowshoes even adorned the hearth.

After a few more trips up North, more two-dimensional art covered our walls. We found a few native artists who did classic stylized animals, the type ordinarily found on totem poles, and then some who created lovely sketches of the animals those represented, juxtaposing the two. Finally, we found sources for wonderful animal carvings, flat on the back plaque-style to be hung on walls. A heron, eagle, otter, crane, orca, bear, and two raven's head dancer masks enhanced our collection. These new additions lined the stairwell leading up to the upper family room/hobby area.

I hit the jackpot when up for a visit to Washington without Jeff. Shauna had given birth to Zarek, her second son, just a couple of months prior to this trip. A day or two after I arrived, she saw an ad in the paper for an estate sale of several hundred items that weekend. Would I be interested? Of course! We got there early for the viewing that Saturday morning, and it became clear after just a few minutes that staying and buying several of the lots would be desirable. Ward offered to watch Zarek for the day, and Shauna and I scurried around writing down the numbers of the lots we would want to bid on.

While I did very well, I could have done better had it not been for the presence of a tall comedian known for his improv abilities. This gentleman, although I was not calling him that on that particular day, lives on Lake Samish nearby and apparently loves Northwest First Nations art. If he began to join the bidding, Shauna would encourage me to drop out. My teacher's salary could not compete. However, I did manage to obtain over three thousand dollars worth of Tlingit and other native baskets, jewelry and nuggets, some arrowheads and other tools, a blanket of the Ganado design and some other trinkets, all while checking in several times with Jeff on the cell phone, frantically describing and giving information and asking permission, which he gave freely.

One of the items I purchased at this auction has remained a mystery. I have searched online and cannot locate anything like it. A basket, it is a large cradle with a fairly open weave, so I was assuming it was a Southwest design — air flow would be needed in the warmer weather. Or it is possible it isn't a cradle at all, but a carrier of some sort and what it would be carrying would need to remain dry and would not be something with small pieces. In any case, it works great as a book and magazine holder next to my bed.

One of the latest pieces I received, an unexpected gift from Jeff, was one I had longed for since I first saw one in a picture — the classic squash blossom necklace. I hadn't thought we could afford one, but Jeff was in the right place at the right time — a train station jewelry kiosk waiting to depart for home after the long high-adventure Boy Scout hike in New Mexico. My husband had said he was admiring some of the pieces when the man in charge mentioned that he was going to be discontinuing that display. Jeff said he probably didn't have time to look, because the train was going to be leaving soon, but that he had always wanted to get me a squash blossom necklace. The man considered, as Jeff headed for the door, and then called out, "Half price." Jeff swiveled and got out his wallet.

For my part, I had a chance to return the favor a few months later. Shauna and her family and I had gone to Vancouver, BC for a day trip early that spring, and my husband hadn't been able to join us that time, stuck at work back home. With our décor and his preferences in mind, I had entered the Native American art shop, momentarily taken aback by the authenticity that flowed out from every gigantically tall wall, every colossal and minute piece of history within. There was a distinct odor of a preserved peoples there. I had been to this place before, but every time was a museum experience.

On one wall leading up a staircase I noticed a form I hadn't seen before: carved paddles. Some were tiny, others oversized, and there were all the gradations in between. I passed by one a couple of times, but kept returning to it. I could make out the stylized animals in their garb of black and red paint on cedar. The piece was fairly new, and it was signed. There was none of the garish turquoise color that, I felt, marred some of the pieces in the store. This paddle was finely detailed, quiet and reassured. I chose it and a few other items — some etched two-dimensional prints with similar stylized animals with their realistic ancestors sharing natural scenes and a couple of trinkets — and had them boxed for travel.

In the end, it was decided I would leave them at my daughter's house, since my husband would be driving back up with me in the summer. It would be an easy thing to pack the box up in the Explorer, along with whatever else we had discovered during that trip. There would be plenty of room in the back — unless we bought furniture, which didn't seem likely at that point. Having lived in that Southern California house for over thirty years, all that remained to be decorated was wall space, and not much of that was left. Still, the paddle, at least, would be a unique addition to the rest of the artifacts we had collected over the years.

After the Canadian excursion, I had a chance to visit the downtown Bellingham shops and discovered two more pieces by a local artist, from whom we had already bought two items. Her specialty was inking and pressing dead sea animals. Since Hubby was a scientist, with a BA in biology, and a frustrated Cousteau follower, this gal's work had appealed to him. He had already framed her coho yearlings and an octopus. It seemed natural to grab the rockfish and the shrimp when they presented themselves at the frame shop. He could build and finish two more nice frames for these, too.

And so I left them all behind — the paddle, the animals, the trinkets — knowing that we could bring them back home that summer. Just in time for our anniversary, our thirty-third, Jeff would open the box and chuckle over what I had collected for him, for our house.

I flash on the items still at Shauna's house. Perhaps she can ship them to us if we can't make the drive this summer…

That had been such a pleasant shopping trip. I wonder how much of it was because Jeff wasn't with us.

My husband is an intensely private man. He is uncomfortable giving out any information for identification purposes at stores. In fact, he can become quite hostile to shop clerks if they even ask him for his zip code. He has stopped frequenting places where more information is requested than the previous times he had shopped there.

I find this very embarrassing. I try to explain to him that if he feels the clerks are out of line, or if he is upset at the intrusion, he should speak to the manager, not the poor minimum wage person working the register, who certainly hadn't set the policy. But since he is usually too angry at that point to speak to anyone politely, he just slams down the credit card or simply leaves without purchasing anything, leaving me mumbling apologies in his wake. I am to the point where I try to forestall the whole situation by moving in front of him and paying myself, or, if it is too late, walking slowly towards the door as though I am just going to wait for him there. This is a very common event, and very unsettling for me.

It is interesting, because Jeff is generally an affable person. But he views store clerks as — I don't know — enemies? I come to dread shopping with him.

The Eighth Night

I journal nothing today. The pages are blank, in part because Shauna and I are very busy going in and out of Jeff's room as the technicians and specialists need us to, and also because we are exhausted. Lack of proper sleep, sleeping sitting up, being awakened over and over by all of the chiming and humming of the equipment surrounding Jeff and others up and down the hallways, people coming and going both from Jeff's room and the waiting area, and because our minds are telling us to always be on the alert. I begin to think that even if I were to sleep, it wouldn't be the restful kind I am used to. I can get by on perhaps five to six hours a night at home when I have to, but here my sleep is interrupted every few minutes by sound and movement.

As a result, my thought patterns vary from the norm. I seem to live more in the moment, sometimes in a near fight-or-flight state, especially when getting ready for a transition, such as going back to Jeff's room after being out front downstairs on my cell phone, or getting ready for a doctor visit. I've always been pretty good about keeping up a calm demeanor, but on the inside my mind is churning, flinging out random thoughts, or zoning out due to sleeplessness.

Jeff is no longer awake. He is sedated due to some secondary stroke activity, and his medications have been changed. The respiratory therapist stops coming, since Jeff is not conscious and can't respond to commands. More tubes, and different types of them, seem to have sprouted from his body every time we re-enter the room. I marvel at the potential cost of electricity generated from all of the equipment in just this room and mentally try to multiply that out by the number of rooms on this floor. The utility bills at this hospital must be staggering. And imagine the wiring inside the walls to ensure that there is never a fuse blown from all of these outlets! The amount of energy needed to maintain a person's body overwhelms me. Each new wire and tube serves to convince me that it will always be like this – that Jeff's body will not be able to regain the ability to sustain itself without all of this medical apparatus. One by one these mechanisms are turning my husband into a zombie. He relies on them for his life. How long will this go on?

Jeff is the scientist, not me. I cannot fathom all of the systems in his body, their workings, and how the doctors and nurses have memorized all of it, accounted for individual differences and continuous changes, and learned how to instantaneously adjust their thinking. The problem solving skills contained in this one facility are beyond me.

Jeff's degree was in biology. He worked as a chemist, but living things were his number one interest. Anything else in science was just a step behind that initial love.

This love was demonstrated in a number of ways. The changes my body went through during pregnancy fascinated him, as did labor and delivery. He was a good helpmate during those times, and a competent labor coach who kept me calm and focused. He also enjoyed examining the baby and placenta along with the doctor. No aspect of biology was out of bounds for him.

Once we got the house in Chino and he had all that yard space as a blank canvas, he was able to carve out some landscaping on his own. Trees and plants which produced fruit or vegetables were of primary interest. He planned out the front and back yards carefully, including sections for a vegetable garden in the back, a grape arbor along the fence, and fruit trees in both yards. Of course, he harvested and processed the produce as well, fearless when it came to any form of food preservation, including canning, drying, freezing and cooking said produce. But one of his real loves was orchids and he had some affection, from a distance, for cacti. So the only way to really nurture delicate items of that nature was to build a greenhouse. For weeks he plotted, planned and sought out prices on the supplies and materials he would need to construct a sturdy room of about ten feet square. Using redwood which he applied creosote to and corrugated fiberglass, a heater, a fan and a mist system, he built a beautiful, fully functional greenhouse in a corner of the backyard. In it were shelves and workbench-type structures housing several varieties of orchids, including a bearing vanilla bean type, and cacti of many species. Jeff enjoyed visiting this area each evening after work, ensuring that the temperature was kept within a certain strict range. He had devised a pop-up section in the ceiling of the structure which would go up when the temperature reached a certain upward limit, and a fan would come on to cool the place off. The mister was on a timer. And on cold evenings the heater would activate to prevent any frost from destroying his beauties.

My husband had a great affinity for animals as well— well, at least several different species of them. He adored dogs, especially ones of decent size, and they him. Anywhere he went, if there was a dog, they interacted. He loved playing with them, petting them, snoozing with them and watching them play. When it came to canines, he was their bud.

Both Jeff and I had always had dogs, and his mom's sister had access to a darling male Sheltie named Tommy who needed a new home. While this dog had a tendency to be somewhat high-strung, especially on trash collection days, he proved his mettle one night shortly after we got him, when an intruder popped out a screen from a window on the side of the house and hopped onto a desk holding a swamp cooler. The second his feet hit the floor, Tommy went off. He was so intent on getting out of our bedroom that he inadvertently threw himself against the bedroom door, slamming it shut. He continued to bark frantically, however, so we staggered out of bed to see what had set him off. By the time Jeff opened the bedroom door, we could hear the front door squeak open. Jeff made it down the long hallway, and then I heard him quietly say, "Shit." The front door was still standing open, with Tommy continuing to yelp just inside the doorframe. Footprints in the newly seeded front yard told the tale of the quick getaway. Jeff and I decided that putting up a fence with locked gates would be the next order of business, and that we would always have a dog.

Tommy remained skittish about things such as car rides, trash trucks and thunderstorms, alternately screaming and hiding between our headboard and the wall behind it during the latter two. He was the dog our girls grew up with, although he vastly preferred adults. A favorite part of his routine was the time right after I fixed breakfast for Jeff and me, packed his lunch and saw him off to work. I would grab my cup of coffee and the LA Times and head for the recliner. Tommy could hardly wait for me to get there, pacing nearby impatiently. The second I was in the chair, he was on my lap. Later, as he grew older, sick with testicular cancer and somewhat addled at sixteen, he would jump into the recliner before I had quite gotten there, and then looked around, confused, knowing something wasn't right but with no idea how to fix it. When we finally made the determination that he was too ill to continue, it was Jeff who held him as the vet filled the needle, Jeff who spoke softly to him and stroked him until he breathed his last. I sat sobbing in the waiting room, unable to attend my dog's death.

Not long after we lost Tommy, a good friend of mine, Sally, who gathered kids and dogs and cats as others might collect Hummel figurines, told me that her Sheltie was about to give birth. Excited once again at the opportunity to own another of these sweet and lovely animals, we reserved one, and eight weeks later went over to pick up Bridget. Following in her predecessor's footsteps, she threw up in the car during the mile and a half ride home. We guessed it must be a trait of Shelties to be carsick no matter how short the distance traveled. Bridget lasted fifteen years, and was primarily Jeff, Jr.'s dog during their early years. Jeff and I let her go too long before finally working up the courage to have her put down. Jeff didn't stay with her as he had with Tommy. Jeff had a true affinity for dogs, far more than for any other animal.

CATs, on the other hand…not so much. A huge part of the lack of interest in cats had to do with the fact that he was allergic to them. Another was their aloofness. The neediness of dogs, their reliance on us for survival, and their abject adoration of Jeff made it easy to love them back. But most cats wandering around outside just bugged him because they pooped in his flower beds and didn't even leave a tip. Me? I would chat with kitties, answering them back in kind when they meowed at me and petting them if they came up for a rub against my legs. But Jeff was more likely to smear engine grease on them if they were on the driveway when he was working on a car. He regarded them as additional rags for cleaning his hands. He wasn't cruel to them or hurtful, but didn't mind smearing up their fur if they got too close. Jeremie recalls a time when he was cleaning off a paint roller and tested its spotlessness on a passing cat.

Now, you have to know this. Sometimes the cat was not even approaching Jeff. Occasionally a cat could be within his view and be called over gently, only to get pets via paintbrushes or dirty rags. He had little respect for kitties.

However, there were a few exceptions. If a cat were assisting him in eradicating the yard of gophers, it got a piece of meat as a reward and petting like a normal person would. So — cats as mercenaries, OK. Cats as pets, no.

Birds were acceptable because of their personalities. Like dogs, they needed people for survival if they were kept as pets, but they made interesting noises and were fun to observe. Howard found a bird, an African cheeked parrot (smaller than a cockatiel, but bigger than a parakeet) in his fig tree in the backyard of his house one day. Clearly, it had been a pet, but had somehow gotten away. Howard took the bird in, put it in an unused cage that had been kept in the garage, and figured out what it needed to eat. No one ever claimed this bird. We soon found out why.

This animal, which the gals in our family called "Lucifer", hated women. It was an avian misogynist. In fact, Howard, Brad and Jeff were the only people who were ever allowed to touch it, and it showed its affection for them effusively by grooming their pelts and facial hair and snuggling into their collars. The women in the family could feed this pet and change the dirty cage papers, but only if fingers and all other body parts were moved swiftly and removed from the bird's reach immediately. I even gave it the end of my cereal from a spoon or allowed it to perch on my empty ice cream bowl to clean up the last bits, but it never returned the affectionate gestures. It attempted to kill me every chance it got, flying after me, chasing me across the floor, screeching the whole time. If Jeff entered the room, it would coo and look cute. Me? Screaming and abuse. Jeremie, when she moved back in with us for a time, would egg it on mercilessly, since trying to make up to the bird was futile. "LOOOO-CIFER!!!!" she would call out when she saw him, and he would feather up and go into Rambo mode.

By the way, the only reason the bird would be at our house was when Jean and Howard were going to be away from home for several days. Otherwise, he stayed with them, thank God. I had no desire to be continually abused by caregiving a lunatic.

We took a large white rabbit from Jeff's sister, Diane, once, and it lived in a hutch on a garden workbench in the side yard, in the shade. This particular bunny, which we called "Blanca", had been used in a lab for testing makeup ingredients. Once the veins in its ears closed off, it was no longer of any use to the company, so Diane rescued it and brought it to us. I don't recall Jeff interacting with the rabbit all that much. Mostly it was amusing for the girls to visit it in the yard. It lived out the remainder of its life with us, and after it was gone, another bunny hopped into our lives, right into our front yard. We couldn't find the owner, so Smoky joined our ranks for a short time. I cannot for the life of me recall what its fate was.

Now, Jeff had developed a carpool for our area, and filled up his car daily as he drove around picking up Unocal workers from different departments. One of the gals who shared the ride lived just north of us on a ranchette of about two acres. The two of them made a plan to use part of her acreage for raising cattle for a year, then they would share or sell the animals for food. Jeff would do feedings once a day, and Milly the other feeding. What we found out during that year included the following:

If you decide to keep large animals on a dirt lot, it will rain more that year than any other in the town's history.

Because of all that unusual moisture, the animals will all develop pneumonia which will require shots of an antibiotic twice a day.

Once the animals are given a shot, they will stampede to avoid you every other time you come at them.

Milly will need you to be the one to give them all those shots.

Within a few weeks, they will get sick again.

Cows are incredibly stupid otherwise. When you drive your old, rusty truck into their area to offload hay or other feed, they will chew on the bumper and headlights.

The geese who live in an adjacent yard will come at you hissing every time you arrive and will not let up until your vehicle is out of sight.

Your wife will not want to see the slides you took of the slaughter at the end of the year.

Everyone will love the meat you harvest. It will disappear far more quickly than you would have thought. You work for a year and get a few weeks of bliss.

We took two of the head at the end of a year, Milly took some, and we parted out the rest. While the meat was extremely lean and tasty, it wound up being a heck of a lot of work for Jeff. This was not an experiment we decided to repeat.

The other experiences Jeff had with animals, predominantly, were to preserve them in formaldehyde. A piranha he had had as a pet, some other smaller fish he had raised, and a tarantula he had trapped while driving through Carbon Canyon — it had been crossing the road ahead of him — occupied large mayonnaise jars in the garage. In addition, he had a few moths and flowers pressed between sections of newspaper and sandwiched between some boards held together with clamps.

Living things, and dead formerly living things, fascinated Jeff. He loved the systems that

created them, that nurtured them, and that eventually failed them. I suppose, as an exten-
sion of that, he wound up being interested in all things mechanical, in building, in creating
a structure, in that the laws of physics come into play — more systems, more rules and laws
to make things work as a cohesive unit.

Jeff was a putterer who enjoyed thinking about, then beginning projects around our house.
Sometimes he even finished them.

One of the first of these events was a playhouse for the girls. Now you have to understand
that across the entire length of the back of our property was a ditch, and the fence between
our house and the church behind us was on church property, which was taller than the land
our place stood on. Putting in a retaining wall to even out our property would have cost
a couple of thousand dollars, even back in the seventies, so that was certainly outside our
budget, with me still staying at home with the kids. So gardens left off at the ditch, the dog
couldn't go down there, and neither could the kids. About six or eight feet along the back
limits of our land was unusable.

And that was significant, because this was a tract home on the minimal lot size for that
time in Southern California. Our home was rather small — four bedrooms (or three and
a den, with the den's double doors leading out into the non-sizeable living room) and two
bathrooms, with no family room. We had tried having the girls bunk together and have
one of the bedrooms as a playroom, but often that resulted in said playroom mainly being a
repository of all of their toys, with little in the way of organization for them, and continual
accusations and counter-accusations of blame for the mess. They needed a place to play
outside, to move some of their belongings out there and get the neighborhood playmates out
of the house. The simple swingset could occupy them all for only a few minutes at a time.

So Jeff began to plan out a playhouse for them. It could have been a single-story structure
out on the lawn or near the garden, but he started to think about how to reduce the impact
on the small backyard and use some of the lost square footage over the ditch. What resulted
was a cantilevered affair, a story-and-a-half house on stilts with the front porch resting on
the flat yard, an unreachable partial loft (we seriously didn't want the girls climbing up
there, but figured as long as we were building, we might want to use that space for storage
later on down the line, so going up made sense), and Dutch doors. The windows became
problematic after live testing due to the need to keep wasps out and yet have some ventila-
tion. But the place was a hit. To little kids, it looked huge. It was created and painted to
look like a barn out there in our back forty — square feet. Many tea parties and clubhouse
activities took place there over the next few years, and my sanity was briefly restored. Our
girls felt it was much cooler than any other outdoor play space in the neighborhood, until
the neighbors put in an above-ground pool.

Jeff also created that amazing yet small greenhouse adjacent to the playhouse. Jeff also enjoyed hydrotherapy, getting out and watering everything in the evenings after arriving home from Unocal- less to hydrate the plants, more to reduce his stress and decompress after work.

Hubby had many other projects over the years – rebuilding his 1960 Triumph 3-A, helping his dad and brother with the '66 ½ Mustang that we eventually bought from his father, maintaining his fruit tree orchard of two apricot, three plum and one nectarine trees scattered in the front and back yards, pruning and fussing over a mini-vineyard that stretched along the rear and side walls of the backyard (after we finally built that retaining wall), sewing down comforters, sleeping bags, snow gear and jackets for use while hiking/camping/cross-country skiing, and picking fruit and vegetables and preserving them through canning, freezing or drying. He taught me much of what I know now about sewing and food preservation – some of which he learned from his mom, and other skills he picked up on his own from reading. He had a lovely collection of science fiction novels, and once we got cable he glommed onto Discovery, TLC and History channels, as well as the old standby public television. Classical music or Monty Python skits could be heard as he worked on model railroad kits or built ship models.

The piece de resistance, of course, was that double family room.

We subbed out as little of the work as possible, enlisting Jeff's brother and occasionally our neighbor to help out. The Douglas fir beams that would extend north to south along the roof of the lower story of the family room were twenty-four feet long. Now you have to understand that this section of the dwelling was being constructed not only by amateurs, but amateurs with little equipment, a few friends and several six-packs of beer. Also, the beams were still quite damp, as evidenced by their somewhat green appearance. This meant that not only were they still green, as opposed to having been dried, but also that they had absorbed many, many pounds of water. So imagine, if you will, three men who have never done this before, each with perhaps two beers under his belt, with two rather rickety ladders. Also, please consider that one of the men was six feet, three inches tall, and that the other two were just over five and a half feet each. So if the tall man hefts up a three hundred pound, twenty-four foot long stick of wood, how much of that weight is on the shoulder of the shorter man on its opposite end? And what about the guy two rungs up on the household-grade aluminum ladder who is about to receive delivery of said beam?

In general, I chose not to do the math. I went into the kitchen and made sandwiches, and babysat these men's children.

So I never saw the very large and wide plywood sway braces swinging in the wind before they got tacked into the upper story support beams, nor my brother-in-law belaying out on climbing rope to finish putting in the remaining nails, two of them per running foot, on the outside of those braces. THEN they started working up on the roof.

However, I did get a gem of a task: a few weeks involving three sessions of sanding and varnishing the Douglas fir beams and pine shiplap ceiling of the first story of the family room, which measured about twenty-five by twenty-two feet. Ensuring adequate ventilation became a must; even then I had some woozy afternoons.

Installing the two fireplace inserts was fun, too. We used the old Egyptian method of lead pipes as rollers as we trucked the pieces through the side yard after they were delivered. It took several neighborhood volunteers and their kids to accomplish that goal, with the kids grabbing the pipes after each large, heavy box had cleared them and then running up to the front edge and laying them down on the ground. Of course, they found it a hoot and were completely willing to make a game of it.

The more-than-a-thousand day effort was well-worth it. In the end, we spent far more time in the main floor family room than anywhere else in the house, watching TV, enjoying the fire, or tucked into the back corner of the room next to the under-stairwell storage closet — the perfect reading/napping corner. The Christmas tree had a much larger spot there than it had had in the living room, and during the holidays we now had plenty of room for extended family members. The big raised hearth, with its flagstone finish and large plank mantel, provided additional seating for us and our dog (Bridget, at that point), and a gorgeous focal point for the room. The upstairs section was transformed into a hobby area for Jeff, later business storage as well. Its fireplace boasted herringbone brickwork that was as attractive as its stone counterpart downstairs. Jeff had a metal business desk he had bought used and its twin metal two-shelf bookcase, as well as the drafting table and workbench with magnifying light. The sewing machine stood ready in the corner. Jeff spent many hours in his lofty hobby space, engaged in a project or three. The lovely lattice-covered deck we had built, overlooking the park across the street and the church parking lot behind us, was largely unused, unfortunately. The upstairs space simply was never used by family as a gathering area. I did enjoy checking out the guys playing basketball in the round court as I dusted up there, however.

Jeff's creative powers didn't sleep during the holidays. For several Christmases he devised nefarious methods of wrapping presents with the intent of fooling the recipients. His masterpiece was disguising Shauna's softball mitt. He encased it in an oversized box, installing a metal pipe leaning over at one end, then covered the whole affair in festive paper. Many out-in-left-field guesses were entertained before the thing was finally unwrapped. Another time, it was box-within-a-box-within-a-box, each one beautifully wrapped. Something very tiny — what it was, exactly, I can't recall — perhaps a giftcard — was the final prize in the center of it all. A scavenger hunt with several notes leading the way was the result of a purchase impossible to wrap — a bike, I think. But nearly every year when the kids were young enough to appreciate it, someone had to work to find out what the present was.

During the period of time he was unemployed, after the Unocal Science and Technology layoffs, he began to really take his time to get into dinner preparations. For several weeks I would come home from a long day of teaching and stop myself at the front door, exhaling. Then I would slowly open the door and inhale, deeply, savoring whatever delightful cooking odors lay within, guessing at their source. Never having been a real cook, only having worked from tested recipes with little deviation from them, it was always amazing to me what Jeff could come up with. For me, not having to come up with dinner ideas during that time was absolutely wonderful. It made it really okay to just confine myself to the mindless cleanup.

This also heralded the advent of Jeff's increasing interest in grocery shopping, particularly at food club warehouses. A Sam's Club or Costco outing typically set us back over two hundred dollars, but the results were heavenly. He rarely worked from a list, so we often wound up with a pantry full of pasta and its requisite sauces, a dozen cans of stewed tomatoes, and an overflowing freezer. In the end, we transformed a hallway linen closet into an additional pantry, since we didn't really need it for extra linens anyway. And the house continued to evolve into what we needed it to be, little resembling those up and down the block both inside and out.

There is too much sitting here. Sitting and waiting. And waiting for news which isn't getting any better.

In the waiting room, in the hospital room, the temperature is the same all the time. Cold.

If you are a woman, you probably understand the need for warmth. Oh, sure, you'll experience hot flashes, possibly, or live somewhere it gets unbearably hot, but in general women have a need for warmth — in relationships, through their skin. We seem to feel the cold more than men do.

I remember feeling cold in my house in the mornings when I was a young child. We had two wall heaters that provided the only sources of heat — one in the hallway between my parents' doorway and mine, and a double-sided one several feet away from that between the living room and kitchen/family room — and I can recall standing in front of one of them trying to warm up, willing the fan not to turn off. There was no thermostat, so you would just turn the knob and heat the place up until someone complained. During the days of everyone wanting straight hair, when I was an idiot in college, I stood too close to one of those wall heaters and singed a section of my long, blonde hair. Horrified, I saw several long yellow tresses stuck in the brush. So I lived with a singed ridge above my ear and thinner hair on that side as a lesson. Back in the day...before blow dryers.

After moving out, there was a time when I lived with my two girlfriends in a triplex over a garage. For some reason I was terribly cold one evening when Jeff was visiting, and he was mystified that I would need to turn the heat up to 72. Prior to that we lived in a dilapidated old house a hairsbreadth from demolition. Luckily, we moved out within six weeks, or I am sure we would have frozen to the wood floor in front of the non-functional fireplace. Remember, this was in Southern California, so how cold could it have been? But I felt every nanodegree below seventy, it seemed.

After Jeff built the two family rooms at the Chino house, each with its own fireplace, there were opportunities for cozying up to a roaring fire. Well, the one in the lower family room roared. The gas one upstairs couldn't even crackle, although it did have a fan to spread the heat throughout the space more efficiently. But both lent a sense of primitive warmth that a central furnace just can't. For one thing, there is the visual — the licking flames, constantly changing shape and configuration. And in the wood-burning fireplace we could ignite aromatic logs and make the flames climb up to the top of the enclosure. So for psychological reasons, a fireplace appeals to me. I am glad my house here in Washington has one — and its being gas makes it easy to manage. It even works in the frequent power outages we get here due to high winds. Once we went for a couple of very cold days warmed up just fine with that little gas fireplace.

My son is currently installing a portable radiator in our vacation house in Union. Shauna and Ward worried that the temps in the twenties the next couple of nights could freeze pipes, and we had no way of knowing whether they were well-insulated or not, since last winter was a pansy. The main house there has a lovely wood-burning stove and a gigantic stack of firewood left by the former owner. A fan kicks on of its own accord after some time and sends the lovely heat throughout the house. You can even cook on the top of it, if you want

144

to — a real boon in power outage times. We've barbequed during outages in Washington, even in the snow. Also, the frigid temps make for an awesome outdoor freezer in case you're worried about losing perishable food.

But today I feel chilled to the bone. It is 23 degrees outside, and I have upped the ante on the heater to 68, as well as turned on the gas fireplace in the living room where I am sitting typing this. I also went upstairs and traded sweaters for an old oversized blue wool one that used to be Jeremie's, layered over a cotton turtleneck, and I have on part wool socks and booty slippers. But after we were out in that cold running errands, then spent several minutes shoveling the lower part of the driveway, and I got shaky worrying about Jeremie driving her non-all-wheel-drive older vehicle with no snow tires (and I was in the car coaching her on the hilly parts), that did it for my metabolism. Even my down REI jacket and wooly gloves didn't help out there. Is it the cold or the shakiness from being scared? I can't tell. Might be a combination of all the physical and mental strain from this morning.

It's strange how that happens. Once we get chilly or start trembling, not a whole lot seems to help. Typing seems to be helping my fingers a bit, though. But this reminds me of the times I had fevers and simply could never get warm, could never break that bone-chilled feeling. Oh, now I am noticing how warm this laptop is getting the fronts of my thighs… good to keep typing.

My sensations of warmth and cold haven't always been in synch with the rest of the world. Generally I would need to have more layers on to feel warm, especially if I were on a diet. The smaller I got, the colder I felt. This makes sense, but even when I am at my heaviest I feel colder than those around me. When we vacationed up in the mountains, and certainly if we were camping out, I would get too miserable to sleep. And yet I never could go to sleep if Jeff were touching me, or trying just to snuggle. He jumped around and jerked as he was drifting off, and that would startle me enough to not be able to relax, awaiting his next pattern of jerkiness. So even if I were feeling cold at night, cuddling wouldn't help me get to sleep. Extra blankets were the only answer. It was a godsend when Jeff put together the down comforter, and after we got a heavy wool blanket from Pendleton. Only if I were weighed down and had the thick loft of down above me could I fall asleep happy. Jeff, of course, had to fling those extra covers off, and longed to be able to leave a window open in the bedroom. I think in my case some of the benefit I feel is due to the whole swaddling angle. Maybe inside I'm still a baby in need of bundling up.

Aside from fevers, the other times I was inconsolably cold had to do with hormones — either adrenaline or female. The first occurred during usual fight-or-flight types of experiences, and also after childbirth. Those bouts of shivering were miserable, but were at the same time a welcome signal that pregnancy was over, and the baby and I were well. Near accidents in the car would bring about a delayed reaction of shaking, again of relief that disaster had not actually struck. Issues with low blood sugar would occasionally do it, too.

Once when I was about 34, I was mysteriously cold. While we were vacationing in Big Bear with our girls and Brad, Donna and their new baby, Greg, I became overly tired and had no interest in going outside at all. The food in the cafeteria seemed to taste odd — my sense of taste was heightened. My sense of smell grew more sensitive. And I absolutely could not get warm enough.

Of course, I was pregnant with a son. Didn't know it at the time, hadn't planned it, but I was about a month along. So the interaction of Jeffy's male hormones with my female ones was causing me to have some weird experiences, certainly not of the type I had had when I was carrying the girls.

The other hormonal experience of a similar type was when I was menopausal. While other women have hot flashes, mine were the opposite — bouts of extreme cold. I might as well have been living in an igloo. Trying not to inflict my frigidity on the rest of the residents of my house or classroom, I simply layered more clothing or used wool more often. My silk long underwear came out of the back of the drawers. Sometimes I would wear it to bed, because it seemed to insulate me far better than my thicker flannel jammies.

(Jeff enjoyed one aspect of the senior retreat of my female organs, at least. I became horrendously horny, repeatedly so. He was happy to help me with that side effect.)

So the cold today has several sources — the extreme cold weather, the wind, the fright, low blood sugar. So I sit by the fire with a little bowl of pecans in my wool sweater, cozy socks and slippers, I have heated up some coffee Jeffy made earlier. I am doing what I can to make things better.

And tonight, I will pull up the dark blue wool blanket, cover myself with the down comforter covered in a new duvet, snuggle with my dog and hope for some warmth. But even though I will be the right temperature for a good night of sleep, the emptiness of my bed transmits a chill of loneliness that never goes away, and that cannot be remedied by deep blankets or snoring dogs.

I realize that I feel cold not because it is terribly cool in this hospital, but because I am sitting too much. I am too tired. I am becoming emotionally exhausted. It is always so nice, two or three times a day, to go outside and lean on the high stone planter just in front of the large, glass front doors, soaking up the heat of the rock the sun stored there during the day. But I only sense it peripherally, because I am on my cell phone filling in relatives and colleagues, passing on news which isn't getting any better. The sunshine is wan, struggling to get through the Los Angeles smog of late May. But I can shrug off my sweater for a few minutes and feel the gift of life going on around me, unfettered by wires and tubes, free to move around in the world. Healthy. Normal.

Shauna is enjoying being outside. In her current neck of the woods, the Pacific Northwest, it is still rainy and quite cool. While she adores her new home, she longs for visits back down here to California, to where it is generally warm, and often hot, all year long.

The media stress the desire for snow at Christmastime. Santa is dressed for it. Even Back-to-School sales tout Eastern and Northern clothing weights and styles, so it is just a matter of accessorizing with some striped scarves and knit hats. Stories of old tell of children longing for a toy instead of the requisite heavy wool coat they know they need. Frosty the Snowman lives near a community wrapped in icicles and glacial scenery. A one-horse open sleigh carries carolers through a winter wonderland. And children everywhere sing songs referencing all of this, mindlessly.

How do I know this? Because I was born in Long Beach, California, and lived in Southern California all my life, never seeing a snowflake until my grandfather ensured I would when I was about 13 and we were driving near Nevada on our way to Scotty's Castle. He killed two birds with one stone that trip, giving my first dusting of snow and having me spend the night in another state for the first time. And yet I memorized all of those old favorites, jingle belling along with the rest of the kids who had never seen a sled, let alone a sleigh. I adored the impending holiday cheer, and joined whatever choir I could to participate in caroling. Some of the lyrics were quite senseless to me, because I had no frame of reference for them. Luckily, the religious songs were supplied with plenty of pictures, and used simple language to convey the holy scenes. And all of that took place very far away both in geography and time.

When you live in a place where it stays pretty warm most of the year, and Christmas time is coming, you learn to fake it. Decorations help convince you that Santa's warm clothing is just the thing, even though people at the mall have tank tops under their leather jackets and are red-faced and sweating. Colorful scarves over tight t-shirts and shorts don't quite cut it, but in the arid inland valley, you have to give a nod to the season.

So you think about pine trees and decorate your house with fir boughs, even though they dry and fall apart after two weeks due to the utter lack of humidity. Paper and glitter snowflakes dangle and sway gently, blown by the breeze from the air conditioner. Tinsel is the closest thing we will ever get to actual icicles.

In Chino, we had several years where what we got for Thanksgiving was ash fall from the brush fires in the nearby hills and mountainsides, ash blown by sustained sixty mile per hour Santa Ana winds which were hot and dusty. By Christmas, if we hadn't gotten much rain, those same hills were dry and brown, and the air remained arid. All of the foliage was parched. It was not out of the ordinary to have temperatures in the 80s as we completed our Christmas shopping and made fudge to give to neighbors. And, again, this is not in synch with the traditional Christmas pictures on greeting cards or TV ads, and there aren't many carols celebrating the high temps on our holidays.

I recall several Christmases when we were hosting dinner for the relatives. Jeff and I would get up early and begin chopping and mixing the stuffing ingredients, and he would *prepare the turkey. We would get the oven going and start working on side dishes. By early afternoon the temperature in the kitchen approached unbearable, and yet still we had to repeatedly open up the oven and baste the turkey.*

The thing about Santa Anas is that not only are they hot and dry and yucky, but they also don't allow the marine air to come inland and cool us off in the evenings. The wind pattern is reversed from the usual. So, of course, we would open the windows, at least on the west and north sides of the house, and run fans, hoping for the best. But on holidays, the oven is going all day, being opened and closed to check the progress of the cooking or start baking something else, and it's hard to escape that constant heat, or to cool off the house sufficiently. And the dry heat certainly dries out the Christmas tree in a hurry. If you don't add water to the bucket beneath it daily, you risk having a decorated tinder box in your living room.

Frankly, I don't know why we don't just give in and embrace the diversity of weather patterns for the holiday season. In Australia, Santa dresses for the weather, which is summertime there. His red and white suit is quite abbreviated, with short sleeves and shorts, and instead of attempting to ride a sleigh, he comes in on a surfboard. Makes perfect sense! He IS the Santa needed for that climate and culture, and I will bet he is a damned sight more comfy without a full velour costume. Why do we Californians (and residents of the good old South) insist on copying the pattern of our Northern neighbors? Why NOT write carols about the lack of snow and ice, no need for a sled or hats and scarves? Our hills are brown. The weather outside is frightful, but not in the same way the composer meant. We are wearing tank tops to Christmas dinner this year. Should we continue to be ashamed of that?

Certain customs the Parsons/Nafs enjoy should go on, however silly in the climate of Southern California. For example, the person passing out presents wears a Santa hat. Sometimes we all do, just because. We also decorate ourselves and our pets with the discarded stick-on bows from gifts we have opened. If the Liles contingency is around, there will be Christmas carols accompanied by guitar. Parsons? Mostly classical CDs, or possibly parody. Nafs? Maybe jazz. There will definitely be a tree, artificial if at Brad's house, due to Greg's severe fir allergy, Otherwise the tree might be living, or cut by a family members from a tree farm nearby. An annual tradition we've started up here in Washington is to make an appointment at a local glass blower's shop to make glass ornaments for the tree. And my grandson, Zarek, enjoys dragging the family off to a religious service Christmas Eve. He was especially fascinated by the lit candles we all got to hold as we sang and prayed in a small church on Vashon Island, where his other grandparents live.

The Parsons like to make a big deal of Christmas morning. We gather at Brad's or my house and cook up a nice breakfast — eggs, toast with homemade jam, and some coffee cakes or pastries, also homemade, orange juice and lots of coffee. After eating and doing a little cleanup, we retire to the living area and start in with opening presents. We try to do this slowly enough so that everyone can enjoy seeing others open what they were given.

This is where the wearing of the Santa hats comes in. It's an important job to read the tags and pass out presents, and the kids feel very grown up when they have finally gotten old enough to share in this responsibility. Later, the home baked goodies and more coffee come out, and soon we are all comatose from the excitement, overeating and sugaring up. Some sandwiches or cheese and crackers save the day, unless a regular turkey dinner is planned. Lately, with the aging of the grandparents, the day is called with sandwich and music time.

For my parents, it was Christmas Eve — dinner, music, opening gifts and carefully wrapping up the tissue and ribbon for another time. Stockings were also part of the ritual, with my mom stuffing the embroidered stockings with things like pocket tissues, chapstick, perhaps a pair of socks and candy. It's interesting that my kids always looked forward to the simple things Mom tucked into those homemade stockings. Of course, there was always one for the dog, too, filled with bones and toys.

When I was younger, I could always count on Nanny to give me pajamas for Christmas, usually flannel. Like my kids with their stockings from my Mom, I miss Nanny's way of warming me up at night that would last me until the next Christmas.

Whatever the weather, traditions in our two families never changed much. Hot or not-so-hot, windy or calm, we always celebrated Christmas in the same way each year. Shauna introduced thematic giving to the mix after she married Ward, and that added to the excitement of opening presents — what would their running gag be that year? Or will it be a more serious effort to give events and experiences in lieu of objects which gather dust? This past year Shauna, Ward and I bought a vacation house together. There's a good chance that this new venue will bring about some new traditions that, if we all approve, will get incorporated in Christmas celebrations to come. I definitely see more shellfish in the Naf's future menus.

I have to say, I prefer living where not only will the trees around me will not be able to go up in smoke due to their being saturated by the constant rain, but also where there is a likelihood of a truly white Christmas every year. In fact, it can get downright frigid by Thanksgiving. The frost definitely is on the pumpkin at that point in the year, the snow tires are pulled out of the garage and mounted on the car, the patio furniture is in until late spring, and it feels and smells the way I have heard about in carols my whole life. This is what it is to have seasons. We absolutely need those parkas, knitwear and caps. We have graduated from the paper ornaments to the real thing. Perhaps my new license plate frame will claim that my other car…is a sleigh.

The Ninth Night

From the yellow journal:
8:30 a.m.

Our lives are now counted in AS – after stroke. Each day brings change, and not always, in fact, rarely, for the better.

Two days ago Jeff had a silent stroke. Vessels vibrated uselessly for an unspecified period of time in his cerebellum, the area controlling balance and coordination. He has little strength in his right side, now. An attempt was made to remove the ventilator. Jeff gamely attempted to work on breathing exercises, but wound up unable to cough adequately to clear the lungs of dangerous buildup, and stopped breathing. Just as I was lifting the receiver on the phone outside the intensive care unit to get permission to return after a brief bathroom break, I got a quick response of "We need five more minutes." Then the call went out "CODE BLUE SEVENTH FLOOR ICU." I peeked through the section window and saw the rush of personnel heading for Room 706 – Jeff's room. Unwilling to watch, I made myself walk back to the waiting room, numb. Looking at Jeff's brother and his wife, I muttered, "It's Jeff."

Again, another scare, but it was only the breathing, easily remedied with the ventilator. His heart pounds on, strong in the face of the disaster going on above it.

Jeff is now sedated – has been for a day and a half. He has a new catheter in his chest and sensors within it to measure and calibrate the massive infusions of liquids intended to force, with the help of somewhat high blood pressure levels (140-160 systolic) hydration into his brain. The leak of the original blood vessel that burst still exists, but it is constantly being drained away by the hollow bolt, and the remainder of his brain is being more suffused with blood from capillaries being forced to work harder. Every effort is being made to ensure that there are no more strokes, and that he doesn't lose any more cells.

Here is the list of support systems:

> three catheters, two with sensors and monitors

> eight IV drips – one open tube for liquids to go to the stomach

seven separate machines and monitors

daily chest X-rays and brain sonograms

hourly respiratory therapy when he is conscious

team of doctors from the neurosurgeons to the pulmonary specialists, as well as general

dietitian (tube feeding for now)

continuous nursing care with meticulous hourly record keeping and narrative reports,

with each nurse being assigned only two patients, and medications are constantly being adjusted

Although I look forward to the day when he can be awakened again, I dread what ground we may discover he has lost. Our lives have been irrevocably changed. Our future is on hold and yet absolutely always in motion.

An important note: I could not do this alone. My wonderful, generous daughter, Shauna, is with me constantly, responding to my every need, voiced or not. She promises to stay indefinitely, putting her own life on the back burner. Her husband and his extended family have stepped up to the plate, as well as her colleagues, to cover for her in her absence. I feel selfish for needing her so much right now, but after seven days of going it alone my reserves gave out. I can't seem to go night after night on zero to four hours of interrupted sleep here in ICU. They provide a comfy chair and blankets, but monitors clanging and the continuous buzz of personnel make deep sleep impossible. Getting flat for seven hours last night at the Omni Hotel was a precious gift.

10:30 a.m. The team of doctors just arrived to evaluate Jeff. It is likely that his brain has swollen due to the two blows it has suffered. The neurologist uses the term, "highly disabled". As the discussion goes on, Jeff's blood pressure drops to 92 over 36. In the case of severe swelling, the doctor discusses what would be needed now to "save" Jeff. I have to wonder what we would be saving him FOR. What is there left of the man I married?

11:00 a.m. CAT scan in half an hour. Arterial catheter to be inserted after, in his arm, to determine second by second blood pressure. The scan will determine the amount of brain swelling and/or vasospasming – the useless pulsing of blood vessels, which no longer deliver an adequate quantity of oxygen-infused blood to all parts of the brain. Potential angioplasty (balloon insertion in spasming part of the brain).

11:07 a.m. Nope. CT scan – innovative technology done here only – in concert with an MRI. Much is going on in the back of Jeff's brain, and this set of diagnostic studies will provide very accurate information. Diagnoses and procedures seem to change by the second.

11:50 a.m. Shauna and I take turns placing calls outside, since we want to ensure that one of us remains on the ICU floor if there is any word of a change in Jeff's condition or a change in plans for him, and one of us needs to go downstairs and out front to place cell phone calls. Basically we are mothballing the troops. This does not look good. Frankly, I am about out of hope. I told Jeff this last week, when he was conscious, that I loved him. I probably told him that more times in the last several days than I have in the last several years. We had a good talk about our relationship, and I hope I was able to relate to him how committed I was and am to deepening it, to making sure we spent more time together. At the time, I was focusing on meal prep and exercise, working toward a healthier lifestyle. But that additional time together would have strengthened our bond as well.

Now I am thinking we will never get that chance. I only wish we had had the opportunity to know Jeff's general health was deteriorating before it all came to this. His stubbornness about going to doctors, coupled with my reluctance to nag him about anything, resulted in where we are today. Life's all about choices. We can't go back and alter any of this; all we can do is learn.

12:59 p.m. They just rolled him down the hall for the tests.

2:10 p.m. He was just rolled back down the hall again. Tests over.

Lack of sleep and a greater lack of good news about my husband is beginning to send me into a dark place. Gradually I am slipping into some negative areas, and I am making mountains out of molehills, worrying about not only the here and now, but the long gone.

A couple of decades ago the term "high maintenance" came into vogue. For a time, I worried that maybe I myself was hard to please, or too demanding. When I finally voiced that concern to my husband, the surprise on his face told me what I needed to know.

Thing is, what we actually give voice to is not always what we feel.

While making love, I wanted to be satisfied but wasn't, so I pretended. For months. When the result of that was that I avoided sex and put Jeff off, I had to tell him why. He felt awful, and I knew I had been completely unfair to him, never giving him a chance to fix things. When we first moved to Chino, I wanted air conditioning in the worst way. It would have been far too expensive, so I didn't complain. We bought a swamp cooler and, later, a tiny one-room air conditioner for the living room, and used some box fans. We also did everything we could in terms of insulation, filming windows and making thermal-backed drapes, which we kept closed during the day. We finally upgraded the furnace and got central AC when Jeffy was about 3 – fifteen years later. I wanted nice clothes, so I bought them for the girls whenever we could afford it, remembering how it was when I started school and had three outfits I alternated for months.

So I probably couldn't be compared to the folks on reality TV shows in terms of high maintenance. But that didn't mean I didn't want stuff. I just didn't ask.

My husband, I have to say, was quite low maintenance himself. He never seemed to be uncomfortable about anything – pain, what kind of food I served (mostly), clothing, vehicles, our house – He just kinda cruised along with whatever we had. He did, however, do a bang-up job of saving up and being frugal. If we needed to buy a new appliance or car, he did months of research to determine the best buy for the money, the one which would last the longest and be what we needed. If we could build or make something ourselves, something of decent quality, that was what we did. We rarely ate out. We went to movies perhaps twice a year. Entertainment was TV and whatever outings we had with scouts, with our kids. Staycation was the norm. Camping came in second, or car trips in the southwest. (I did a typo, and this next sentence began with a dollar sign. Coincidence?) Even when our income was higher, when I worked, he was still very careful. He simply was not a demanding man. His needs were hardly quantifiable. He was able to save because he didn't need to spend.

Mainly, the financial sacrifices we made had to do with the limits imposed on a single-income family. We agreed for me to stay home with the girls until they were in school all day because both of us felt at the outset that that was what was best for them. There is little point in whining about that now, thirty-plus years later, and there is no way to know any harm that might have been done them had I worked. I mean, my mom worked and I turned out fine, but I LONGED for her, you know? I didn't want to come home to an empty house, or to go to someone else's house when I was too young to fend for myself.

Having Nanny there for the few years it made a difference to me was a nice thing, but she wasn't Mom.

What worries me is this: since I wasn't completely happy being stuck at home, there, I've said it, and when I did get to have a career it was SO fulfilling, then was it really the best thing for my daughters that I stayed home with them? Could they tell I was bored? Did I stifle and smother them by always being around? Were they relieved when I finally went to work?

Being somewhat histrionic, although I HAVE gotten better over the years, pretty much means that my maintenance level was higher than it would have been for someone calmer. I am pretty sure there is a connection there.

Of our kids, Jeffy was the easiest to cope with. I am not sure how much of that is because he is a boy, and how much of it was because he has a lot of his dad's qualities. As a baby, he had a sunny, easy disposition. Just don't stop feeding him to wipe his mouth, as his Auntie Diane found out one day. Being a neatnik, she noticed he was drooling out some of his baby food and went to clean him up a bit after just a few bites. He let her know in no uncertain terms how unacceptable that was. "OK! OK!" she repeated as, per my advice, she just shoveled it in. Sated, all was well. Only partly sated, not so much. Getting him to sleep was not that tough, either. He had his dinosaur stuffy, one of us sat on the floor by his bed, and he went off to dreamland. Unfortunately, so did we, perhaps a third of the time. With Jeffy, stick to a routine, it's all good. And he was pretty easily entertained, as well. See, I don't know how much of all that I am saying was because I was with him fewer days a week, since I went to work half time right away with him, and I was with the girls full-time, or maybe it's because he was the third, so little surprised me. In any case, it seemed as though having him last worked the best, because of my starting to teach.

Something in our lives that did change fairly dramatically after Jeffy was born was that we had a teenager in the house, and, three years later, another one. And both female. And who did they mostly butt heads with, aside from each other? Me. The other female in the house.

With Shauna, I always felt it was because we thought quite similarly. And we both were/are control freaks. So it was all about who was going to be dominant. Yet I loved her fiercely, probably in part because she was so strong. Until she hit college, we had many days when things were miserable. So, around one another, we were both high maintenance.

Jeremie was another story. Always fragile and sensitive, she was someone I tried to get to toughen up. I worried that she lived in her sister's shadow. In the end, it was more about my domineering ways that messed her up, I discovered when she was in therapy after having toyed with the idea of killing herself, and Shauna had caught her. Shauna made her write a letter to us explaining exactly what was going through her mind when she picked up the razor blade.

Shauna and Jeremie have had many differences over the years. While I feel Shauna needs to lighten up and let the past go, I also feel that Jeremie owes Shauna thanks for having stopped her that day.

All three of us have struggled with our weight over the years. I wonder what we are feeding.

It was probably a good thing that they had both moved out by the time I hit menopause.

All marriages seem to have tidal changes, ebbs and flows of the passion, the connection, the understanding, the commitment. Jeff's and mine certainly had a lot of that.

People used to comment on the fact that we never fought. There was a reason for that. Jeff didn't feel all that strongly about things, and if I did, I said nothing. So there. No fights. Not a good thing, but at least it sounded peaceful.

I am the kind of person who avoids confrontation. When viewing an argument, my tendency is to walk away, even if I don't know the persons involved. I hated having to attend school board meetings, and I won't go to my homeowners' association general meetings, because I KNOW there will be conflict. I don't mind differences of opinion, but can't stand the raw emotion and lashing out that come with being around people who won't listen. When my own children would begin yelling or crying in frustration when I was correcting them, I would leave the room. Reason is all, in my book. And when you have reasoned arguments, you can reach a resolution, or at least agree to disagree. For someone as domineering as I used to be at home and, initially, in my classroom, I rejected non-logical argument. A proper debate should not involve putdowns. You can present your point of view in a manner that doesn't devalue the person or persons you are giving it to.

I feel that way to this day. So the political rhetoric, especially around election time, leaves me cold. Give me good, hard data and a logical conclusion based on historical and accurate facts, and I'm yours.

When Jeff and I actually fought, about once every eighteen months, it wasn't about reason, initially, so I hated it. Jeff would blow up and punch a wall, usually avoiding a stud and creating a hole in the drywall, and I would completely back off and get quiet, knowing that he was too angry, seeing red. Then I would vigorously throw myself into housework, clattering pans around. A few hours later, I would go to him to try to deal with whatever we disagreed on, and immediately break into tears, which I hated, because that meant I was permitting emotion to reign. Eventually we might work out a couple of points. In the end, it was still dysfunctional, because the little stuff we needed to work on continually got shoved under the rug until it built up to a boiling point. I see myself still behaving in this manner to this day, with my kids. But understanding that this doesn't really work and figuring out how to change it, or having the courage to be assertive on a daily basis isn't something I am ready to do, apparently.

I had similar dealings with Shauna, where we would butt heads and stop talking for a time. The resolutions never seemed very satisfactory, though, and it was rare when either one of us would admit any wrongdoing. I had an incident with her that mirrored the one I had had with my own dad — when I sobbed to her that we had to figure out a way to stop treating one another so badly. To this day, I often feel as though I am walking on eggshells around her, weighing every word to avoid a reaction from her. I have never found out the best way for us to take care of our disagreements that doesn't leave me feeling nervous and ill at ease.

When my kids were young, and when I was dealing with situations in the classroom, I never left small issues unresolved. In fact, I rather micromanaged. When it came to the bigger stuff with teenagers, how they were doing in school and whether they were following house rules, I pretty much kept them in lockstep as much as possible. But that pattern got broken with Jeremie, whose therapist told me to back off on issues of school and food, because although she might still be heavy and failing high school in a year, she would still be alive. When Jeffy began taking his passive-aggressive stance to an artform in the upper grades, I began to feel that nothing we did, positively or negatively, no matter how consistently we enforced rules, would ever make a difference. His senior English teacher reported exactly that — Jeffy was a self-motivated learner and nothing extrinsic would change how he was doing at school. For a teacher, that is a hard aspect to approach. So for the last two kids, I had to let go of school-related issues: for the middle child, so she could work on her emotional problems, and for the youngest because it wouldn't make a difference.

Jeremie didn't graduate from high school, but earned her GED the following year. She was stunned at how easy that wound up being. It killed me driving home from school and seeing kids trying on their caps and gowns and getting photos taken. I felt like I had failed her, and didn't know how to fix that. How to fix HER. Jeffy graduated, but began to flounder at community college. He hadn't been all that successful within a more structured environment, and yet all the freedom of college didn't seem to make a difference, either. I recalled what his English teacher had told me — it wasn't about ANYTHING outside of Jeff's mind. Where he was, who the professor was, what the subject matter was — it was whether he made a connection with any of it.

Sometimes he did, with spectacular results. If it was a teacher or professor he admired, or a topic he found fascinating, it was all good. If the person doing the instructing was boring or flawed, the subject matter couldn't make up for that. Sometimes I found that with Jeremie, too — she often did well even in a difficult subject if the teacher showed that he or she believed in her, or if she were grouped with children she enjoyed being with, and they were doing well.

And both of the latter two children DID wind up making a connection with drugs, which brought them camaraderie with others around the fringes of the community, of the educational experience. For Jeremie, it wound up being more important, more of a connection for her, than anything else. For ten years, she flitted in and out of our lives, our home. We kicked her out three times, and then said there would be no more chances.

Jeffy managed to keep afloat, just, in college, and didn't steal from us, so he stayed on. His specialty was car wrecking.

First he laid the car his dad had bought from the leasing agent that had lent him this car for his work on railroad tracks at ten o'clock at night. A black car in the dark on railroad tracks. He called, petrified. He had been racing and playing chicken with another young driver in an industrial parking lot in Pomona. They were good high school band kids, ferrying others home, when someone got the idea to play this dangerous game. When he hit the tracks, veering off to avoid hitting the other boy head-on, so much dust was kicked up that, briefly, he thought the car was on fire. He and his passenger managed to get out and survey the damage — broken axle and other issues. I reminded him that he had a triple A card in his wallet, and to make the call, as well as to talk to anyone he could locate that worked on those rails. Then his dad and I took off to see how things were going there. Jeffy did manage to get someone to come out and remove the vehicle, and, luckily, no trains were scheduled on that track at that hour of the night. The tow truck gentleman, after arriving and checking out the situation, turned to Jeffy and asked him how this had happened. "I was stupid. I fucked up." The man nodded sagely, shook his head and began the process of extricating the car from the dusty tracks. Then our son got to learn how much car parts cost and how to fix those types of injuries on our driveway, with his dad supervising but Jeffy doing all the work — the same thing Shauna had to do with the Mustang when she had rear-ended an off-duty police officer. The car recovered, but not for long.

A few months after, Jeffy was plowing along in the dark in Carbon Canyon (beginning to see a pattern here?) on roads with which he was unfamiliar, but the boy in front of him (different child) DID know well. Jeffy wound up off-roading it and flipping the car upside down in a ravine. Then he had to stop and think, "OK, nothing on me is broken. OK, if I just unbuckle, I am going to hit my head on the ceiling of the car..." This time the car was totaled, and, once again, miraculously no one was hurt. Given our son's recurring pattern of luck, the insurance company gave him more money than we had bought the car for, so he had extra to spend on another vehicle, since bus systems in Southern California suck and he still had to get to college.

Neither one of those wrecks involved drugs or alcohol, to my knowledge, but the wreck Jeff got into with a fireplace hearth did. After imbibing quite a bit in a short time at a buddy's home, he got up and then fell into a brick hearth and broke his nose, sustaining a bit of a concussion. Thing with that incident was, we didn't find out about any of it, including the few hours in the hospital emergency room, until the following morning when Shauna and I went to wake him in his bed and found him swollen and in bandages.

Some people seem to have to learn by doing, rather than take advice or watch the downfalls of others. My younger two have been like that. However, both have survived, both seem to be putting their lives back together, and we still have a decent relationship. With my oldest, I learned not to criticize, because she felt very solidly in the right and didn't want to be corrected or reminded. No conflict with her was ever productive. So, in all cases with my kids, it was I who had to learn how to deal.

My connection with others now runs the gamut from withdrawal to desperation. I am physically in the room with them, or on the phone appearing to speak and take part in conversation, but rampaging fatigue is clearly affecting how I interact with others. My school colleague Sally would say, "It's time to get flat." I haven't been in a place I could do that for days. Shauna and I need to head to the Omni Hotel tonight, the closest one of an acceptable cleanliness and safety level, and actually lie down in a bed and sleep. Flatness is what I need.

What is it about men and chairs? I would be willing to bet it was a man who designed those sitting places, and yet I have never known a man who could just sit comfortably in one for more than four minutes.

Jeff, his dad and his brother all affected a similar slouching pattern in chairs. You could probably photograph them over the course of an hour and see the same postures over and over again in the three. Aside from having the same basic torso length (longish, considering their lack of stature), the same rather short legs, the overmuscled arms and strong shoulders, they used those parts in very much the same way. These men were clones, one would swear. They thought the same, they watched the same kinds of shows on TV, they were men of science and math, and they slouched the same in any kind of chair. My mother-in-law sketched my husband once, perhaps a year or two before I met him. He was slouched in a corner of the couch watching some science show on TV, his chin resting on the back of his hand, wrist at a ninety degree angle as though it had been dislocated, hair disheveled, floating alpha waves. The man's a sponge, but a champion sloucher.

Did I mention that sciatica runs in that family?

Yeah, I won't soon forget the time my second daughter arrived at my school to let me know that Hubby was flat on his back on the garage floor and could not get up. Having wrenched his back while twisting to the side to set a box down, he had experienced a spasm that knocked him flat. Luckily, as I said, we lived in Southern California, so he wouldn't freeze to death out there, but that had to be pretty uncomfortable. As soon as I was able to get someone to take my class, I ran home (two blocks — I know you envy my commute!) and helplessly wrung my hands, unable to be of any real help. After perhaps an hour of unsuccessful attempts at rising, he was finally able to do a slow crawl into the attached living room and pull himself up to a chair I steadied for him. Eventually, he made it to the kitchen. I stuck a cordless phone in his hand and fled back to my classroom.

Did I mention that my husband was not necessarily all that pleasant to be around after he had injured himself? Consumed not only by pain, but, worse, by the anger that resulted in his feeling that he had brought this on himself, the rage at helplessness, and the frustration of forced inactivity, as well as the inconvenience of having some task interrupted, which meant he wouldn't be able to finish…

Oh, WAIT A MINUTE! Did I mention that our home was FILLED with unfinished projects? So it couldn't have been anger about THAT — that was a constant!

I remember the time he had been working on metal out in that very same garage and had lacerated his cornea. It was clear to me that he needed to see a doctor. He was in pain, there was no way for me to medicate an injury of that type, and HE NEEDED TO GO TO THE DOCTOR.

Oh, wait. I already told you how much he hated to go to the doctor, didn't I?

Now I know what you are probably thinking, having stayed with me this far into the narrative. You are assuming that I was in a miserable marriage with a grouchy, slouchy brilliant nerdy guy. Well. Yes and no.

I was sometimes miserable. I was sometimes on edge. I often shushed the children to keep things quiet and peaceful when Jeff was home. I tried to keep the place clean. I tried to serve balanced meals (looking back, they might have been balanced, but they sure were boring). I watched his shows on TV with him, at least initially. I suppressed a lot of myself, especially in the early years of our marriage. Why I couldn't just cut loose and be myself, I have no idea. When I finally worked up the courage to tell him all the stuff I just told you in the last paragraph, he was puzzled. Stunned. Had not realized at all the efforts I made to be the person I thought he wanted me to be. He asked me why I had done all that. Why I had changed my behavior. He had married me for who I was; it never occurred to him that I would feel the need to turn into someone else.

Thing was, maybe once a year Jeff would go into a rage. Normally the event which precipitated this would be minor, but there would have been a LOT of those minor events over the course of the previous weeks to which he would not have reacted. Usually this outburst would culminate with his putting his fist through a wall. At no time could I reason with him while this was going on, although the logician, the mother, the teacher in me would attempt it. So I would generally flee. I would clam up. Only hours later could there be anything approaching a remedy, or closure. I would cry. I would be frustrated. And I would resolve internally to avoid another encounter of this nature at all costs.

Perhaps I don't even need to mention how much I loathe conflict.

So by the time we hit close to thirty-three years of marriage, I was pretty much into just smoothing things over, or disappearing to fling myself into housework, or jamming down disappointment and unrest. By the time we got to May 14, 2005, I would be in the den on the internet reading, writing or editing or discussing Star Wars fanfiction with others around the world while Jeff watched his shows in the family room half a house away. By the time we had been married for over three decades and spent more than half our lives together, we were both working fifty-five hours a week, had raised two-thirds of our kids and had grown pretty damned far apart under one roof. We never argued, because we didn't talk much. We were rarely intimate, because we went to bed at separate times. We chose to spend our precious free time apart. In two years, we figured, we could retire. Secretly, I hoped we could grow closer, perhaps, once our vocational obligations had been met. Maybe, once the job pressure was off and we had relocated to a cooler, calmer place, we could commune both with nature and with one another. I dreamed of that day.

The nightmare which occurred is one from which I am slowly awakening, and from which Jeff possibly never will.

At one point during the afternoon I go into a funk where few of the decisions I made in the past make sense, where several activities I was involved in appear to be wastes of time, and connections I thought were critical to my creative flow were one-sided, at best. A fandom friend I adored is perhaps only a handful of miles away, but either cannot or will not call. A mutual friend tells me that she contacted this gal to let her know what has occurred with my family; surely since she had met Jeff, she would be moved to call or send an email. Again I am reminded who I should be focusing on in my life.

Years ago I was asked to be the matron of honor at a wedding to be held on the other side of the country. Now I enjoyed the friendship of the couple through fandom connections, and had recommended they both join a website, where they met and fell in love. All of this was virtual – our friendship, their online meeting, emails – yet even when they spoke on the phone and eventually met, they had made that love connection – two lonely people who otherwise would never have known the other existed, conjoined at first by Star Wars.

I flew out for the wedding in the spring, meeting up with another fandom friend and rooming with her. She was on furlough from the Marines at the time. We met the lovebirds, did some shopping with them, bought wedding presents and went on over to the ceremony, to be held at a nice park in the old town of Spartanburg, South Carolina.

I knew the moment I met them that it was wrong. And so I was catapulted into the position, as someone who was standing up for them, of judge. Should I say something, or butt out and let things unfold without my sage advice?

In the end, I said nothing, although it was blatantly clear that no good was going to come from this union.

Well, I was almost right. A pretty, personable little girl, named after me, sprang from their loins. But the relationship didn't last. Eventually she took the baby and left him. Thank God her parents stepped in and helped her out, since she is employed but not in her college vocation. But I sense she will make it, just as my second daughter has, for her child.

Probably had I spoken up prior to the wedding, they would have married anyway, and I would have lost contact with both of them. I don't think my intervention would have seriously affected the outcome. But there will always be that nagging doubt. On the other hand, perhaps that child having been named after me is the legacy that needed to happen, the little person who will turn at least her mom's life around.

I have a lot of fandom acquaintances. Some of them are semi-dysfunctional and several live on the fringes of society, never quite fitting in, never quite feeling as if they are succeeding at life. There are a few who, like me, have figured out how to make it all work while remaining quirky. But many of us have few friends outside of our given fandom, and are viewed as socially awkward geeks. Quite a few can't seem to maintain relationships, or even establish them in the first place. Many of my online buddies have Asperger's, either identified or suspected. Perhaps because I had students with that disorder, I figured out how to interact with them with some degree of success.

But as I inventory my internet friends lists I see that few of them are married or have children of their own. Some had relationships which are now no more. But the majority of them can't maintain a physical connection, although their virtual ones seem to hang on for years.

And most of the ones that last were with other geeks. I know of only a couple of those bonds which resulted in at least middle class success levels.

And why is that? Well, fandom obsessions eat up a lot of cash for zines and collectibles. Folks who spend a great deal of time on the computer are rarely spending anywhere near that much time building relationships with real life people. And the focus is hardly ever on sustaining and building personal or family fortunes. There is far less vision of the future going on, and less connection with the here and now needs of everyday life. This "perfect world" of a comic, book, movie or TV character, a fantasy life, is more entertaining and engaging. So, even though many geeks heavily involved in fan life are well-educated, attaining high-level degrees, the ability to fully attach to a profession is limited by the overreaching connection to the fandom.

I walked the narrow line of geekdom. Three degrees, two of them in obscure fields. Close ties to fan life online. Yet a husband and kids, extended family and activities. So I stayed up late, learning to live with less sleep, did housework and chores faster, and probably less efficiently, and transferred a lot of the obsession to my job when a key online friendship that had held me in thrall fell apart.

Looking back, it's hard to imagine that level of fixation. But for a period of perhaps eight years, I could hardly wait for the chance to escape into that virtual world. It was more meaningful to me than most of the real life that went on, that I lived through day to day.

Part of it stemmed from my disconnect from my marriage. Another aspect was my demanding job that ate up additional hours of time at home. I craved that perfect character in the fascinating other world dreamed up by someone else. Living through that character, I could always say the right things, be the righteous person, contain more power than any human could imagine, and yet be so conscientious in its use. The stories I wrote in that universe moved people and bonded me, at least for a time, to strangers. Why was it that those unseen could sway me where folks with whom I shared space could not?

With the help of some who had the expertise, I built a website, an enclave for budding authors, a safe space for us to nurture one another's efforts in fanfiction. Every day I would look forward eagerly to the conversations that took place there. My evenings were filled with story arcs, "plot bunnies" (tangents), and talks with other fanfiction authors. We carefully critiqued one another's works, occasionally tread on toes, yet worked it out. The website held a literature section plus a gallery for fanart. While it was true that I kept out trolls and naysayers, nevertheless the number of functional people participating seemed higher than the strugglers. Before one of the major crashes of the site, the couple that I had "introduced" had their wedding pictures posted there.

It's all gone now, destroyed by a spammer/bot and my lack of website expertise. But it was gone for me long before. I haven't felt a real need for any of it for years. Most of the relationships I had in the fandom have slowly fallen apart, and none of the players, including me, seem all that interested in reclaiming any of it. People drift apart in real life, too. It's OK. And that perfect character can certainly live on in the imaginations of others. It's especially nice to see him admired by my grandsons.

Even the man who played him has let him go. The man who created him…never really knew him, I think. He was one of us — the dysfunctional geeks of Star Wars. Much like the Trekkers and the Whovians, and all of the other fanfiction freaks, the collectors and artists, striving for something better than the life they were forced to be at least a little a part of.

So tonight I mull over the fallout from not having said what was on my mind. And the geek within me ponders about what power I really do have over others. The histrionic part of my psyche, the part that ruled those years ago, is really sure I could have made a difference. But the sixty-year-old-plus grandma knows better.

Losing my friend those years ago changed my life. It turned me inward and made me morose, crying in the car alone on trips down to my parents' house, reading into song lyrics stuff no composer ever had in mind. But losing Jeff? Finally, would I figure out what really mattered?

On the drive to the Omni I am mulling over how my relationship with Jeff needs to change, how our life together must alter course. It isn't just the food, drink, and inactivity. It isn't only Jeff's job stress. It isn't the kids. It's us.

For years I have taken my husband for granted. I know he will never stray, but what am I doing to actively keep him interested? Throughout our marriage it has been my perspective that I am the one to make the first move, to bridge the gap, to close the chasm. If so, then I am the member of this duo who has allowed the crack to develop in the first place, and permitted it to widen. I watched it happen, not caring to make the effort to throw Jeff a rope. It was easy to reason that I had never really known him, not all that well – that he closed himself up so tightly that it was impossible to get in. It was a simple matter to immerse myself in my job with the excuse that he should want the best possible education for ANY child, not just his own. And my work on my website is GOOD work, creative and helpful. I provide a nurturing place for writers rejected by "the system". Some of them are very good.

Why is it so easy to allocate my time and energy anywhere except hearth and home? The husband of a colleague of mine had lamented to her, "THEY get the very best of you. You have nothing left for us when you come home." Some of us educators nodded our heads, having heard similar statements from our own families. To my knowledge, few of us ever changed a thing, simply echoing education journal articles claiming that this is the life of a dedicated teacher's family.

Perhaps I am going to have to leave the classroom, turn off the computer, sit with my husband and listen to the TV shows, or the records, or the silence he prefers, in order to make a start on finding him again.

*There was one particularly dark episode of Jeff's rages which none of us — his girls or me —
will ever forget. Shauna was probably ten, with Jeremie being maybe seven. The two of them
were out in front of the house arguing about a red bike chain. As soon as their dad came
home Jeremie asked him to mediate. His response was to take the chain, throw it on the
roof and declare, "There! That's solved!" In the garage his anger continued, unabated. He
put a fist through a pegboard-front tool case, threw a metal toolbox against the dryer, then
grabbed a mallet and started in on his TR-3A. The girls came into the house, wide-eyed.*

*Jeff had had issues with anger before, but usually they involved a fist through drywall, then
he would go off in the house and simmer down. This would occur perhaps every year or
year and a half. Lasting only a minute or two, they were frightening, and I did what I
could not to incur them. But this episode went on and on. I grabbed my car keys and the
kids and took off.*

*I had nowhere in mind. There was nothing I needed to get, no errands to run. But I felt
that we needed to be away for at least an hour to give him a chance to cool off. So we went
off to the mall. Jeremie says I bought a record there, perhaps Simon and Garfunkel, and
I recall picking up a J C Penney Catalog. We returned home, and I told the girls to wait
out front until I had determined that the coast was clear.*

*I went in quietly, into the living room slowly. He came out of the kitchen area, looking
ashen. Taking me by the hand wordlessly, he led me out into the backyard, away from the
girls. Jeff had never struck me in any way, so I wasn't really afraid that he might, but I
was unsure as to what was about to happen.*

*I had been able to see only his back as he led me out to the grass. Once there, he turned
around, still holding onto me. Stunned, I realized he was crying.*

*"What happened? What did I do?" he choked out. "I remember coming home, then…noth-
ing. You and the kids were there, and then you were gone."*

*It was surreal. He described how he "woke up" to find us no longer there, so he checked
next door, then drove to one of my friends' houses, then called my mom. Of course, in those
days, there were no cell phones, so all he could do was try to think of where I might flee to.*

*He had completely blacked out during that tantrum. He didn't recall what had precipi-
tated it, what he might have said or done, nor even getting home, actually. After I told
him what I had heard in the garage, we both went and surveyed the damage. Luckily, his
car was not marked, but the pegboard tool cabinet was a dead loss. He was very remorse-
ful, yet scared, too, because he had not only lost every shred of control, but had no memory
of any of it. He realized that he had blown up right afterward, and assumed that I had
taken the girls and left him. His relief at our return was palpable. But I had to tell him*

that if he ever did anything like that again, with that level of intensity and unremitting, blind fury, that I WOULD leave him, that I couldn't allow the girls to witness that or feel afraid of their own father.

However, we found out later that none of it was his fault. Several other employees reported black out episodes during the course of that week. Apparently some chemical had leached into the ventilation system and had caused varying levels of reaction in many of the building's workers, frenzies and blackouts being among the effects. So while it was an isolated, unforeseen event, it made me leery of his anger for years to come.

In general, Jeff and I were pretty dysfunctional when it came to disagreements. I would clam up and do frenetic housework, knowing he would not be able to reason with me while he was mad, and he would put a fist through drywall, luckily only scraping knuckles, and then we wouldn't talk for hours. Finally, I would break the ice, blubbering my way through my anger. Being a mom and a teacher, I was all about resolution. He would have preferred to just forget about it. Our fights were extremely rare, and they were often unproductive. I think, now that I look back on it, that they served to clear the air of tension, but hardly ever made things better in terms of resolving conflict.

When my girls began to have boyfriends and long-term relationships, it disturbed me how disrespectfully they behaved during disagreements. They had never heard that kind of talk from their parents. However, what they did hear and see wasn't necessarily that healthy, either.

The Tenth Night

At this point Shauna leans on me to tell Jeremie how serious things have gotten. She convinces me that Jeremie should be called while there is still time for her to visit her father. It concerns me to discuss how awful the situation is with Jeremie, since she is so close to delivering her baby, and it is a hot drive from Apple Valley. Still, I sense the truth in what Shauna asserts. The call is made, and Jeremie arrives within a couple of hours.

There is no air conditioning in the car she has arrived in, and she is flushed with the weight of her pregnancy and the early onslaught of summer. She and I stand at the foot of Jeff's hospital bed as tears run down her face. Finally, she utters, "That's not my daddy."

I gaze at her father and see through her eyes. Jeff is swollen and discolored, and deeply unconscious. Seemingly random tubes and shunts snake over and around him. Machinery beeps, lights flash on and off, and numbers change and alter color.

"You're right." Did I say it out loud, or did I offer encouragement to make this all OK for my pregnant daughter? Neither of us remembers.

But I know she is right. This is no longer her father. If he wakes up, who will he be?

The remainder of the afternoon, although spent mostly still in the waiting room while Jeff's medical staff works with him and mulls over test results, seems made of movement. Family members come and go, coffee is procured and sipped without noticeable effect. Jeremie is taken back home by her boyfriend; I worry that the whole situation is too stressful for her to deal with right now. There appears to be no progress or reports from ICU, but clearly there is SOMETHING going on in there, because we aren't in there WITH him. At some appointed time, around 5 or 6 pm, I believe, I lift the phone to get permission to go back in to see him. "Just a second..." is the reply. Alarms begin to sound, the claxons heralding cessation of breathing and/or heartbeat. Suddenly I see much rapid activity through a space where the window isn't covered. Personnel are rushing into Jeff's room, and the line on the phone I am still holding goes dead.

I return to the waiting room in a fog. Everyone there has heard the bells and looks up anxiously as I enter. "It's Jeff…" I say softly, although I am sure the look on my face has already told them that.

I don't know how long we wait for a report, but eventually a nurse comes to the waiting room and lets us know that Jeff is hanging on and that his team of doctors is meeting. Hours pass with no new information. Finally, I approach the ICU window again, pick up the phone and ask how my husband is doing, and if anyone has anything new to tell me. It is around 9 pm.

The sweet ICU nurse who has been there for Jeff many nights buzzes me in and directs me to a phone on the counter. A receptionist is calling a member of the neurological team to give me a report. It isn't Dr. T, because he has taken ill, but another neurologist whose name sound familiar. He had been part of a conference with me previously in the week.

Eventually the connection is made, and an apologetic man is at the other end of the line. He carefully explains the steps of the falling dominos, the relentless flowchart process Dr. T had shared with me days before. The pinball of Jeff's fate has dropped where no one wanted it to go.

Jeff has been suffering from a series of strokes caused by the dead blood pooled in his brain. It came to rest in the folds and crevasses of his brain tissue, and the capillaries it touched have had what amounts to an allergic response – the vasospasms of useless, vibrating pumping that doesn't deliver blood adequately. The first stroke, ten days ago, is what is slowly killing my husband. The first brain attack that bathed Jeff's brain in blood, blood that lost contact with life-giving oxygen and nutrients, is causing secondary strokes from which Jeff may never recover.

The doctor gives his regards, I mumble something, and the call has ended. This doesn't sound good at all, with the neurologist painting a picture of severe disability, yet I am left wondering if there is any hope at all of recovery. I need Dr. T to tell me the odds, so I can find a way, however unlikely, for us to get Jeff through this.

After letting the family remaining here know the current prognosis, I and some others go outside and make the requisite calls. We are all still in limbo, but it is getting darker all the time.

Soon I am called back into the ICU desk area. Dr. T, who sounds horrible, is on the phone. "Mrs. Parsons," he begins. "I am so sorry about your husband."

I am stunned. Is this it? I turn to look through the opening of Jeff's room. He is there, the machines still recording his every function. What does Dr. T mean?

"The tests we took this afternoon show that the latest strokes were around Mr. Parsons' brain stem. It no longer functions."

You don't need to be a brain surgeon to know what that means. Jeff will never wake up. His organs will stop working without machinery telling them to. It's over.

Dr. T offers his condolences; the rest of the conversation is short.

I set down the phone, ending the conversation with the neurologist, and wheeled on the nurse who was immediately behind me to my right. "His brain stem's gone. This is stupid. Why are we still doing this?" My voice seemed shrill, at least in my head; it was the first time I had raised my voice in the ten nights since Jeff's stroke. So I worked to modulate my tone and sound a bit more reasonable while the monitors chirped in the room before me, answered by higher-pitched ones down the hallway, the rainforest calls of ICU machinery. "Give me the papers. Show me where to sign. We are ending this. I am not going to let my husband lie in this undignified state. He would never have wanted to live like this." Flashes of him hiking, gardening, BEING…

When our dogs were ailing and clearly at the end of their time on this earth, at least in the physical part of it, we had a tough time reaching the decision to put them down. Why was it so easy, so instantaneous, for me now? Jeff had been the indecisive one, so we had always gone at his pace. There was no warning voice now, slowing down the process. I had no data to look up on the internet, no documents to search for, no one else to consult. "I'm calling his parents. Give me an hour or two to marshal the troops." The nurse smiled at me with warmth and something that looked like gratitude.

I march out of ICU to the waiting room. Peering through the window towards the top of the door, I see another family with children is there. So I motion for Shauna and Donna to come out into the hallway, then close the door.

We step away from the waiting room window, away from the ICU door, to a small alcove, and I take Shauna's hands. "It's over," I say gently. "His brain stem is gone." We melt to the floor in anguish and defeat.

Calls to family are made. His parents, brother and sister will come. Jeffy is on the way. Donna assists me in making sure that all the required paperwork is signed. She moves easily around the medical personnel, having lost her father not all that long ago, and having watched after her mother's surgeries. We let the nurses know who is coming, and to please wait until everyone is there. I have no idea, once the process is begun, how long it takes a person to die.

Some family members will remain in the waiting room during this process. One by one, they come to say their goodbyes while all of the mechanisms keeping Jeff alive whir and click. Jeffy stands with his arms clenched against his chest, struggling to keep in his emotions, but I can see that he understands that this is the last time he would see his father. I pull him to me, and he collapses on me in sobs. I have never heard my son cry like that, and hope to never have reason to again. Jeffy is only nineteen years old; he is at a time when a young man needs his father to help him fully mature into the man he is meant to be. His dad knew him better than any of the rest of us, I felt. I pray that we will be able to help mold my son's final forming without his father's guidance.

"Oh, they're definitely taking care of him," Diane's fireman boyfriend Ron observes, nodding in approval at the IV dripbags decorating one of the poles surrounding the bed. "They're REALLY taking care of him." It is somewhat reassuring to know from someone acquainted with emergency rooms and medications that my husband will be free of pain during his final ordeal. I just desperately hope that he won't be afraid.

Several of the monitors have been disconnected, or, at least, their readouts turned off for those of us who don't need any additional reason to worry about Jeff's condition. With his brainstem gone, high blood pressure will be less of an issue now. His aspirations and exhalations are very loud and deep. And his strong heart pounds on, oblivious to the futility.

Jean and Howard enter the room slowly. Jean's disbelief is palpable, the sounds from her throat guttural, animalistic. Howard briefly sobs, barks out, "It isn't supposed to be this way," clearly referring to the proper order of things. Parents die, THEN children. He squeezes his wife's arm and leaves the room to remain with his younger son in the waiting room. It makes sense, though, that the woman who was with Jeff when he came into the world would stay with him as he leaves it.

In the end, it is just four of us – Jeff's mom, his sister Diane, Shauna and me. I alert the favorite nurse to my mother-in-law's age and condition. Jean is using her cane, leaning on it heavily. My main concern is that she may pass out from grief and hit the hard floor.

Morphine runs into the shunt in Jeff's chest in ever increasing dosages. His breathing is primitive and very labored; every few minutes I soothe his glossy forehead with a cool washcloth. Gradually we gather around him, some of the essential women in his life. I remain near his head, on his right side, touching his chest or hanging onto his hand, trying to murmur words of reassurance as I swab his face, ruddy with effort. His mom is near his feet, stroking his leg as she balances herself on her cane. Several times I can hear throaty moans as Jean comes to grips with losing her oldest son far too young. Across from her at the bottom of the bed stands Jeff's only sister, saying quiet prayers for the big brother she has always revered. And at Jeff's left hand is his first daughter, continuing to stand strong and supportive for all of us.

Each respiration sounds through the room, every one seemingly the last. But another comes, and another. The ante on the morphine is upped, and the work gets harder, and still the heart and the lungs struggle to carry on although the brain is no longer in charge. We hold up one another, and hold onto him, and pray for his body to finally give up.

Thirty-five minutes later, it does. A last, long inhale, and a blowing out of life, and we groan along with it. The color changes, muscles relax, the labor has ended. Less than three hours after I had talked with the lead neurologist on the phone ("I'm so sorry about your husband, Mrs. Parsons" – well THAT certainly was a conversation starter), turned around and asked for whatever it was I needed to sign to end this, and gotten help to marshal the troops, my husband's life is over. I leave his body at USC University Hospital ICU, never to see him again. He has done all the work of dying, and yet I am the one who feels I exerted every ounce of energy I ever had that night.

I'm certain that it's possible that my initial feelings for Jeff were based on lust, on attraction on a mostly physical level. It's not as though I viewed him first and foremost or for an extended period of time as an acquaintance or friend. There was an electric impulse from the beginning. Over time, the urgency of joining and the abject need to be together faded or grew more mellow or comfortable — however you want to express that. There were times when I would have preferred to be alone, or when things were uncomfortable between us. At times I would fantasize about life without him — but he was never replaced in those daydreams by another person. I think, having married so young — I was only 21 — I never really got the chance to celebrate solitude, to commune with myself. I went from my parents' home to living with roommates to living with Jeff to having a family. Only since his death have I spent any length of time in a house or a car on my own. And I can't say as I love that, but I have no need to find anyone else to love, either. At this point I feel I probably never will.

But love did determine the course of my life thus far, and figured heavily in Jeff's. Love brought us together, created three children, and kept us with each other for over thirty years. Love carried us through those times of silence and keeping our backs to one another, through short, inane dialog. I refuse to believe it was simply inertia, because when his doctors finally revealed that his brain stem was gone, I acted promptly and with little thought to what should happen next. Honestly, love guided me to end his body's continuing when there was no further hope of sentiency. Within three hours, his family was gathered and the medications started and disconnection from life support begun. In love, his mother, sister, oldest child and I manned the corners of his bed and guided him gently towards his final moments. No nurse or attendant or doctor stood in the way of that — in fact, they eased the transition for him, for us. The second I put down the phone, ending the conversation from his neurosurgeon, I turned to the charge nurse and asked for the papers I would need to sign to end Jeff's life. I was angry, certainly, and that was clear in my voice as I said, "You show me what I need to sign to end this." And my next sentence expressed what would have been what Jeff would have said to us, "My husband would never have wanted to live like this."

I learned later that many families prolong the suffering of their loved one, asking for a few more days to work things out, some time to get a second opinion, an hour more to hold the sufferer's hand. For me, there was a rush to stop Jeff from merely surviving, from the indignity of complete helplessness, from the vegetative state of brain death. This was, after all, the man in dark sunglasses who had sneaked up on my heart, who had sired my children, a man who climbed mountains and doubled the size of our house and provided for our futures. This was a man who could fix anything but this. He deserved better than lying unconscious forever in a hospital bed tethered by more cords and IV lines than I could count. If he was never going to be able to masquerade as an old man of the sea, telling tall tales to passing children, if there was to be no more brewing of beer and sitting by the fire and road trips with classical music on the radio or Garrison Keillor or Monty Python, no more filthy driveways speckled with car fluids, no more Jeff except in inert body, then the loving thing to do would be to end it — for him.

What is love all about, anyway? I found out. Love is encouraging people to kill your husband when, if given the same choice, he would have done it himself.

Grief

a friend said the loss of a lifemate is
the tearing of a soul
but it is far more than that
it is the hollowing out of a heart
the numbing of thought and emotion
the emptying of purpose and self

keeping busy with mundane activities
perpetuates the myth
of being OK
it is easier to smile when you don't think

I am never going to be OK
it would make no sense to recover
from three and a half decades of love
three children shared
elation and depths of despair
and everything between

grieving is forever
aloneness mirrors his exile
I stare at the copper box and wonder
if he knows
how much
I loved him

The morning after, Jae posts this on my website:

Here's the latest update on Jeff's condition: it's not good. Sue said when I talked to her last night that "There will be no happy endings for this." Jeff had another stroke on Sunday. He is unresponsive except for pupil reactions, and is on a respirator. His team of doctors is among the best in the world, and they are doing everything they can think of. But the phrase being most used among them right now is "highly disabled," and they can't tell Sue whether the disability will be mental or physical or both.

Sue is exhausted, understandably so. She will out of touch with us for the forseeable future, as she has moved into a hotel near the hospital. She's trying to keep her spirits up, and her family has rallied around her, but I can tell that it is starting to wear on her.

As always, please keep Sue and Jeff and their family in your thoughts and prayers. Sue also expressed her concern that we not let the site flounder in her absence, so let's keep writing and posting.

JediJae

And then, an hour later, this:

Bad news - Jeff passed away last night. 😖

Periodically I get up and look out the window at the dark driveway or through the glass facing the back deck, where I've left the light on. I'm waiting for the first snow of winter.

I've waited for a lot of things in my life. Often I don't pursue what I am waiting for. This pending snow had me preparing this week — capping the hose ports, grabbing extra meat and milk at the store, filling the gas tank and having the tires changed out, charging lanterns in case of a power failure, which we have a lot of up here in Northwest Washington. So I am ready, and now I wait. You can't chase snow, call for it, grab it by the throat. The weather has us all in thrall.

When I was small I waited to grow up, so a knight on a horse would come and whisk me away to a fairytale land where everything was perfect, including me. When that didn't come, I went to high school, then on to college, and looked for The One. And I don't just mean that One Degree. I was also hoping for an Mrs. I got both, but only really ran after the academic prize. The other, I waited for, longed for, lusted after. I wasn't the first to reveal my feelings.

Then I awaited the first birthing. Her first smile was a treasure I looked for and worked to earn, but it had to be given. I wanted a house, and waited for Jeff to decide on the one for us all. I wanted my family to grow, and worked with Jeff to make that happen, but, in the end, had to let biology and luck intervene. Then I waited for my chance at a career. Jeff had apparently waited for a son, and never knew his desire until it happened.

After getting my wish for a career, and then working full-time, I counted the days until retirement. Some years I didn't need to count every day; other years I tallied the hours. After Shauna moved to Washington, I looked with Jeff for a good place near her for us to retire to, and we saved our money but Jeff could never settle on a good location. There were many we saw which would have suited me just fine, but I waited for him to be pleased, too. That never happened.

We waited for Jeremie to wake up to her own potential, her future. We waited for Jeffy to do the same.

So we waited for retirement, the perfect date for financial independence. We plotted and saved and recalculated. We were two years away from that goal.

Jeff had his stroke. I waited for him to tell me what he needed, offering a place to lie down and rest, to take him to the doctor. Then I waited for the paramedics after he told me to call 911. I waited on my knees in the living room for them to help him.

I waited outside for my son to drive safely home from work to see if his dad was OK.

180

Jeff waited in the back of the ambulance, posturing, unconscious, in a coma. Deep. Waiting for the doctors at the hospital down the street to decide. Waiting for the helicopter.

Waiting in a packed emergency room for word about my husband. For someone to show up and help me wait. Waiting to call some loved ones because I didn't know what the hell was going on yet and could only report that things were bad.

Waiting all night. Waiting to sleep because I had to tuck my purse behind my legs in the county hospital waiting room, with gangbangers and crying babies and homeless people.

For them to let me see him — five minutes every two hours on the hour. Waiting for the respiratory assistance equipment to be detached so he could talk to me, and I could find out if he still could.

Waiting for him to stop hallucinating so I could get him back to the reality of what had happened to him, where he was. Waiting for his short-term memory to improve so that I wouldn't have to repeat what had happened every few minutes. Waiting for him to stop trying to rip out the IVs, the drain in his head, and get out of bed. Waiting for him to settle down so I could get some rest, too.

Waiting for the truth. Getting sickly smiles and nods instead.

Waiting for the next helicopter transport. Waiting for them to settle him in a new bed, a new hospital. Waiting for tests and diagnoses. For a chance to eat. For time and opportunity to call people and ask them to call others because I didn't have any more time. For the coil embolization procedure to make a difference. For the bleeding to stop. For him to breathe on his own. For the dominoes to fall and the flow chart to resolve to the bottom. For them to let me back in the room after he stopped breathing again. For him to wake up. For him to wake up.

For all of this to stop. For it not to stop. Make it stop.

And then it isn't about waiting; it is about deciding. He can't anymore, won't ever anymore. It's my job now. And it doesn't take an exhalation's time to do it. Make it stop. He wouldn't want to live like this. What do I sign to make it all stop?

The instant he can't do it anymore, I spring into action and am suddenly very decisive.

But then we have to wait for family to arrive. To say their final goodbyes to their dad, their brother, their son, brother-in-law. Then his mother, sister, older daughter and I form a line around his bed after the nurses do their magic, and we wait. I sponge his forehead, we whisper reassuring words to him, his mother groans — a sound I have never heard before from any human being. She carried him in her body, pushed him out and nurtured him, and now she is saying, "It isn't supposed to happen this way. No one should ever have to lose a child. Parents should go first." But she stands with us, feeble as she is, she puts her cane aside and touches his foot covered with a sheet, and waits with us. His sister lost her first husband, and now her big brother is passing away.

And inside I whisper a thanks to the doctors and nurses who never batted an eye when I finally lost it and insisted they tell me where to sign. One of the sweet aides stands by, upping the ante on the morphine. She had explained how it works when you let a loved one go. She had said she admired that I was doing this for Jeff, rather than making him hang on for weeks as some family members in the ICU do even when there is no brain activity and no hope. I knew how Jeff needed to preserve his dignity, and there could be little of that here.

We wait, breathing with him and wanting him to stop. He struggles, primitive breaths now, with little brain function behind it. He perspires, and I mop his brow and whisper that it is OK, he can let go now. There is no need to fight anymore. Just the other day I had told him I needed him to fight, and he needed to cooperate with the doctors and nurses. But now it is OK to stop.

His heart is strong, even if the brain is no longer telling it much. The morphine grows more powerful than the body, finally, and our wait is over with one long, last, shuddering breath. His color changes immediately, and we stroke him for awhile longer to ease his spirit.

We make phone calls. I tell my principal I will not be back that school year. We prepare the house and the food for the wake. I wait for the death certificates and make the phone calls to Social Security, insurance companies, banks, Schwab. I write as many thank-you notes as I can each day. Until I just can't write them anymore.

My students wait for me. I make a couple of appearances, but it is terribly difficult. I know I am letting them down, but it would have been worse to see a trusted adult fall apart and behave anything but professionally. They deserve to have a chance to learn that last six weeks of school.

We all wait for everything to really sink in. I go back to work in July, half-time, thankfully, and get a lovely group of students for that final year. Yet, towards the end of it when the house is cleaned and painted and ready to sell, I can hardly wait to start my new life.

In many respects I still am.

I sip the wine quickly, waiting for the buzz. I suck at the lozenge, waiting to breathe normally after exerting myself in the cold. I wait for Shauna and Jeremie to be civil to each other – talking doesn't help and may even exacerbate the problem. I wait for Jeffy to grow up. I watch for signs that everything is working. And mostly I worry and feel paralyzed, waiting.

In a positive way, I learned to do that in the classroom — wait and see. Sometimes waiting and watching allows folks to work things out for themselves. Not always. Though.

Many nights as I get into bed and turn towards the wall I try to talk to Jeff. I tell him I love him, which I feel I didn't do nearly enough, and I wish him well wherever he is. I hope it is nice there. And I ask him to wait for me. I have to believe that he is. Honestly, I don't care where he is, so long as I can be with him again. Heaven, hell, purgatory, wherever. God or no God. Who the hell cares? I believe in Jeff, and I want to find him again.

Often I feel that that is what I am waiting for.

Over the course of my lifetime I have vacillated in my spiritual nature. For my first nineteen years I was a good Catholic girl, attending Mass every Sunday, keeping up on the sacraments, and listening intently to the sermons delivered from the altar. After having been at college for a couple of years, though, the first questioning time of my life took hold. Everything was suspect. All points of view I had blindly received were now brought to the table.

The war in Vietnam, of course, was the obvious first point of departure, as, for the first time, I was surrounded by every viewpoint on that crucial issue, rather than the one or two presented when I was in high school. Talks among students and professors down in the commons and out in the square, written materials and open-air speeches drowned me in their "facts' — data skewed to a purpose. I knew the truth was in the middle there somewhere, but having been sheltered on the right side of social and political matters, I began to swing over to the left. The women's movement caught hold, and those of us who were a C cup or larger abandoned our bras, yet held our notebooks tightly in front of our jiggling chests as we crossed the campus. Afternoons between classes might find me reciting names of the Vietnam dead over a mic in the sunshine, then handing over the task to another waiting student. Kent State. Rock and Roll with suggestive lyrics sung by a concert band viewed through the marijuana haze.

Jeff.

My values became fluid as I worked to assimilate more information in four years than I had ever learned in the whole of my life.

I regret nothing that I did to figure out the world during that time. To this second, I would trade any number of things to feel Jeff inside of me again as his arms pull me tight against him, that initial nanosecond of joining. The good Catholic girl stopped going to Mass when priests at every church she tried berated youth from the pulpit and decried the destruction of civilization at the hands of the young. The devout maiden went to the Free Clinic and, without remorse, obtained the medication that would ensure barrenness. In an instant, her soul was lost to a mere man.

Whatever.

When Jeff touched my back in that dark concrete stairwell, and, unbeknownst to me, I fell completely in love, my life changed unutterably. Something huge had begun for me, a sea change of epic proportions. And I didn't realize just how much until he died, when that last, long, rattling breath let go and his coloring changed as the blood pooled to the area of his body contacting the hospital bed, and I came to realize that I no longer cared whether I would see the face of God after being permitted through the pearly gates. All I wanted to see after my life was over was Jeff, waiting for me. As I told a Christian friend to her dismay a few weeks after Jeff had passed away, "I don't care if there is a God. I believe in Jeff. I don't care if he is in limbo, heaven, hell, or some as yet unthought of place. I just want to be with him." There was a scarily calm moment driving his Unocal commute through Carbon Canyon's twisty roads when I wondered how much it would hurt if I just continued straight instead of angling with the next curve, when I toyed with stopping the pain abruptly, but my Catholic fear of hell because of suicide (Jeff certainly wouldn't be in hell) and what my violent death would do to my kids and grandkids made me turn the wheel. I didn't ask God to intervene then, for Jesus to take the wheel. I allowed myself in that instant to reason, and made the choice to stay alive on my own.

Where does God figure in things? It doesn't matter to me in the least.

Now that is not to say that I haven't prayed. Just yesterday, after waving goodbye to an old friend, I thanked "God or whoever is listening out there" for sending me good people in my life. In tough situations I ask for help – from whomever. Am I doing all this just in case there is a God? Is it force of habit? All the preconceived notions I had of a deity disappeared without even a poof while I was in college, when the priests turned against my very essence, and when I was presented with a better choice.

What seems to apply now is, as my brother-in-law named it after I described it to him, is more of a Shintoism, a belief that there is life or energy or the Force in all things. It is actually quite similar to Native American philosophies, as they thank the deer or the salmon for helping them survive before they kill them, or the tree for providing shelter for their families or a canoe so they can go fishing before they cut it down. That mindset works for me. And I think it might have even been acceptable to Jeff, who was at least an agnostic, probably atheist.

Where is God? On my death, I will look for Jeff. If they're together, awesome. If not, I'm cool with that. Just give me my husband back.

Boundaries

The buzz from fine wine
The hum from the laptop fan
Silence hanging in the summer darkness
Everything is waiting

The wine has no party, no audience
Only me in a quiet house
Awaiting drowsiness
But Calibri stretches onto the white emptiness

Sleep is fleeting anyway
And dawn will bring a cacophonous chorus
My dog is impatient
Lying at the foot of the stairs,
Snout aiming up
She longs to escape coyotes' distant howls
tiny bat or owl screeching on the wing
all make her restless, yet here she stays

Each night I talk to you
as I settle into my pillow's depths
I know the feeling
The need to move on
The longing to reach past where I am
To where you are

After perhaps an hour or so, when family gradually said their good-byes, promised to call that day (it is after one in the morning), Shauna, Jeffy and I trudge out the front door of USC University Hospital for the last time. Before leaving, I tell the nurses to contact whatever agency harvests organs and tissue and have them take whatever is still usable. Since he was a scientist, it feels right to allow whatever was left and usable after all of the drugs he had been infused with for over a week to be captured and offered to others in need. Jeff, of course, would have wanted to watch those procedures (I wonder if he can??). Due to that decision, cremation seems to be the logical option. Doing that would also permit us to take him with us no matter where we lived. So I give all the pertinent permissions, and the three of us walk out the door.

I have never taken such heavy steps before. Each footstep feels leaden, impossibly heavy. It is as though I were aging years just on the path to the parking lot.

Shauna drives, as she has been doing for most of the time she has been with us the past week.

During the drive east, one of the first things out of my mouth is how much I want to leave. NOW. I want to get away from Southern California, quit my job, abandon the house. Although I feel perfectly reasonable, I know I am being anything but. Shauna reminds me that it is best to wait six months before making a permanent decision after a trauma such as the one we have suffered. Jeffy, in the back seat, is probably horrified that his world will be turned upside down even more. But I have never liked my surroundings – the weather, smog, insufferable traffic, politics. For some reason, it is as though Jeff's death has unfettered me. In reality, I am in fight or flight mode, and since I cannot fight my husband's passing, I want to flee from everything that might have brought it about.

We arrive at an empty house in the dark. All of us are too keyed up to try to relax and get some sleep. Jeffy goes off to his room at some point, and the phone rings. It is after two o'clock in the morning. I answer, thinking it is a family member, but it is the agency in charge of Jeff's body. They want to know if I will talk to them right now about organ harvest, because it is urgent that we act now. Seconds are precious. So for the next hour I answer incredibly detailed questions about my husband's lifestyle, medicines, daily habits, frequency of drinking, sexual routines. I try not to become annoyed at some of the questions, reasoning that there are biological constraints on every iota of information they ask for. Jeff's extreme sense of privacy rears its head, but he is gone now. I respond as well as I can to everything they ask, then request any information they are allowed to give about how the bits and pieces of his corporeal being will be used. Finally, the interview is over. I drop into our bed, exhausted, but able to sleep only fitfully by gripping his pillow tightly against my body, inhaling any hint of scent still trapped there.

And in and out of a year

The next morning we are up early. Shauna is already making a list of preparations for the wake which will take place next Monday, May 30, 2005. I have sent off a few emails to friends, posted on my website and livejournal account. Joe writes this as a response to my blog entry:

My first glimpse into the wonderful mind of Jeff Parsons was in 2001, in the limericks thread at Fanfix, for which he wrote the following:

A smuggler named Han was there once,
And Leia admired his bunce.
Our Han thought her hot,
But Leia said, "Not!
Just go off on your Nerf-herder runs!"

I knew then that you and Jeff were a wonderful couple. Every word I ever heard you speak about him was joyous. The only time I had the pleasure of speaking with him was when he answered the phone the second time I called you. My regret is that I never got the chance to really talk to him. He seemed to be an absolutely wonderful man. And seeing how happy you were every time you spoke about him, I know it's true. And if there is indeed a reward after life for such people, I know that right now, he couldn't be happier.

Sue, you have been one of my most trusted and dear friends since we first met. Friend, mentor, kindred spirit in our shared craft. My heart bleeds for you and your family in this time of sorrow and remembrance. Nothing I could ever say could change anything that has transpired, I know. But just let me say that you are one of the most wonderful people I have ever had the pleasure of knowing, and being your husband, Jeff must also have been very special. I cannot describe the sadness I feel for you and your family at this time, but know that my thoughts are with everyone whose lives Jeff has touched.

Later I receive this email from Dorothy, another fandom friend:

Sue, I was away in England until yesterday when I heard about the death of your beloved hubby.

It took until today for me to be able to form words.

I never met him but from over here he was as much a part of you as your site, your stories, and any other bits that "show" in this virtual community. He may not have posted or spoken up but I always sensed his presence in you and near you. I always identified powerfully with the two of you - we're about the same age, and how many other couples do you know who have been joined at the hip for an adult lifetime and found it wonderful? He was the Jeff whom I envied you for every time you described that night's menu. He was the Jeff I somehow knew was there behind you, supporting you in your work and your hobbies and all your endeavours.

And now suddenly the forces of the universe saw fit to suddenly and swiftly spirit him away from you. You must be howling, "why?" What could they possibly want with him? He was yours, he IS yours and suddenly he's not there with you any longer. It doesn't make any sense, none of this seems to make any sense and my heart has absolutely broken for you and I want to reach through the ether and wrap my arms around you and howl with you.

I do howl with you.

All my love,

Dorothy (Geo3)

His colleagues from Unocal, headed by Ron Lucasiewicz, send their best via email as well. :

On the job, Jeff was well-liked and respected by all of his co-workers. He always enjoyed a challenge and he was as comfortable carrying out the most delicate chemical analyses as working on the plumbing and equipment repair projects… it seemed like Jeff could fix just about anything,, and he really enjoyed doing it, too. In over twenty years of working together, I always admired his cheerful attitude, strong work ethic and pleasant disposition. Over the years, there were many opportunities for Jeff to complain and back away from the hard work, but, admirably, he never did. He was a one of a kind person.

Another coworker, Darrel Gallup, with whom Jeff carpooled for years, sent this:

Jeff was truly a wonderful man, husband and father. I could see that in his everyday living. I enjoyed his friendship and work that he did for me at Brea and in the Philippines when he was consulting. During my medical problems, Jeff chauffeured me to and from work. Had I not had that support, his encouragement, a listening ear and loving spirit to carry me along, I'm not sure where I would be today.

My good Marshall buddy, Ellie Pedersen, offered a poem:

I remember Jeff's welcoming spirit
And the offer for a glass of his homemade wine

I remember Jeff's laugh
His dry sense of humor and witty remarks

I remember Jeff's love for the outdoors
Treks with the Boy Scouts and hikes up Mt. Whitney

I remember discussions of natural disasters
The likelihood and consequences of eruptions, quakes and floods

I remember Jeff's greenhouse
And the backyard pond

I remember Jeff spending the weekends repairing
Computers and cars

I remember Jeff's boundless love for Sue
And adoration for all of his family

I remember
I remember Jeff fondly

And I smile

Neighbors and colleagues call and drop by, asking what they can do to help. One of the moms of a student in my class hauls over enough sandwich makings, chips, drinks and snacks to get us through several days, and wants to do more. I am stunned by the generosity all around us.

Colleagues from my school have organized themselves into groups, by grade level, office and support staff and are taking turns bringing food and restaurant gift cards by every day. The PTA is helping out as well. We will not have to expend any energy food shopping or cooking for the next week.

Jeffy's school professors are trying to work things out with him for the end of the term. Everyone seems to understand the enormity of what has happened to our family.

The folks on my website take up a collection. They are donating money to the Boy Scout council in our area and to the Sierra Club. We decide to let others know that those would be Jeff's wishes, too.

The Wake takes on a life of its own.

Today I am working from the photographs taken at Jeff's wake, May 30, 2005. I think these were the ones Ward took, and they are mounted at A-Larger-World, my Star Wars fanfiction website, in the gallery.

Before the wake there was much to prepare. Aside from the general cleaning frenzy endemic to the days before any large gathering, there was food to plan for, purchase and prepare, getting out the word to anyone who might like to attend, as you would expect. However, in addition to all that, for Jeff's wake we decided to create "centers", similar to the learning centers I had all over my classroom. We wanted people to know Jeff as we did – not only by his personality, but, more importantly, by the projects he was constantly immersed in. So we made a list of them, which Shauna also used for a bookmark-style takeaway – and typed up a short sentence for each, which we then printed out, cut, and glued onto black paper. These we taped around the house after setting up small vignettes.

While I was working on that, Brad and Jeffy were bottling the wine they had found in carboys in the garage, after tasting it fresh from the five-gallon bottles it resided in. Some of it had turned, and was fed to the biosphere. The rest they bottled, a several-step task involving preparing the liter bottles by cleaning them, sometimes also needing to soak off the labels, swishing around some sulfite solution in them, hanging them on a rack to dry, and then filling them with the wine and corking them.

Shauna, in her turn, was designing the wine and beer labels and the program, devising a timeline of Jeff's life for the other side of the bookmark-shaped program, then getting them printed off. She and I had gone out and purchased a leather cover for a notebook and some special paper for mounting photographs inside it. She put this all together and selected photos to glue in. There was plenty of space left on each page for people to write their thoughts, and unique metal-infused inkpens were bought just for that purpose.

When the labels were picked up, Brad and his wife, Donna, carefully glued them onto each bottle of beer and wine Jeff had brewed. The graphic design Shauna had worked on included a stylized Native American sun figure she had partially copied from an artpiece hanging in the stairwell, and a craggy outline of Mt. Whitney before it. Surrounding the outside of the central art design were the words, "Toasting his life."

Ward had arrived with the boys and worked on the landscape and the garage, getting everything he could into shape for the wake. My neighbor Robin was a huge help with just about everything, especially with the lasagna dinner Shauna was preparing.

Meals every day were provided by the Marshall staff, with grade levels and support staff taking turns with that responsibility. Not having to think about dinner preparation removed a big burden from our shoulders. This was a huge assist towards our whipping everything else into shape.

When folks entered the open front door the day of the wake, they signed in and took a program, which reminded them to go all over the house, the garage and back yard to view all of the work Jeff dabbled in over the years. Most of them went back to the kitchen and family room, where many chairs, tables and food and drink areas were set up. Here are some of the "centers" they could visit:

In the garage, the Mustang and TR 3-A were on display, in various states of restoration. People could also see Jeff's large collection of power tools.

Back in the living room Jeff's large collection of science fiction hardbacks were available for perusing.

"You can't be a little old winemaker without a fruit press" said the card next to the beautiful piece of furniture Jeff had made from rock maple and cast iron parts he had bought from a catalog, designing the piece based only on a picture. He and Brad would use the press in the yard, wash it down, let it dry, then return it to its place in the family room. The juice they extracted would almost always eventually be turned into wine, and the pressed fruit leavings joined the compost heap.

The family room itself was a showpiece – Jeff's most intricate and gorgeous creation.

One of the stained glass lamps was featured as an example of yet another art form Jeff had explored. He had made around five in total including the one which hung over the recliner in the family room, and had designs and colored glass for one he had planned to make for Shauna.

The orchids and cacti Jeff had nurtured were to be found in the greenhouse he had designed and constructed in the backyard.

On the landing, the grandfather clock Jeff had built from a kit when Shauna was little gained a lot of attention.

Photo albums of Jeff's Boy Scout treks and Mt. Whitney attempts, as well as model trains and ships were displayed on the upstairs bookcase and hutch he had designed and built specifically for that spot at the top of the staircase. (The miracle? My new house in Washington had an inset in the wall next to the living room fireplace where that piece of furniture fit perfectly.)

Nearby in the upstairs hobby room, a down parka Jeff had assembled from a kit was hung, with the notation that he had made a comforter, more parkas and down jackets, backpacks and sleeping bags for us, as well.

Back downstairs in the family room, an easel held the scrapbook Shauna had assembled, and the pens rested there, too, waiting for folks to record their thoughts. On the hearth atop a Native American design imprinted on a wool blanket rested the hammered copper on red cedar blanket box we had found online at Hill's Native American Crafts – the same place in Vancouver, BC, I had bought his paddle – for Jeff's ashes.

Shauna had made ten batches of lasagna, Jeff's favorite meal, the ingredients for which my colleagues had provided money for purchase. Along with salad and garlic bread, we had fruit pies, another Jeff favorite. Robin continually ran next door and back, bringing back fresh supplies from her fridge and oven. To drink, we had the usual bottled water and sodas, but prominently featured Jeff's beer and wine for all to "toast his spirit". Jeffy and his similarly underaged friends were seen absconding with several bottles...

Dozens of bouquets and plants which had been sent were scattered all over the house. They definitely lent a more cheery tone to what would otherwise have been a completely somber affair.

Attending the event were over one hundred and sixty people – family, friends and neighbors, my colleagues and Jeff's from his different jobs, and many Boy Scout and Cub Scout members and their families. Even a member of my fandom website showed up! Especially heartwarming was the show of support from Jeffy's friends and their parents. Jeffy's buddies took care of him not just by being there, but by "helping" in the way they thought best – providing alcohol and drugs. At one point the kids moved to the park across the street (not coincidentally where Jeff was airlifted from two weeks prior), where, that evening, some police stopped by to check them out. Luckily, the kids were able to convince the officers of their intent to help Jeffy cope with the loss of his dad, and the cops just told everyone to go back to our house. At that point, of course, they had the munchies and descended on the leftover food like a swarm of locusts. When I realized what had gone on over at the park, I mused to myself that I was glad they were all OK, and Shauna, somewhat miffed, wondered why they hadn't shared. ;)

When I had a chance, I wandered over to the scrapbook to see messages loved ones had left there. My brother wrote, "Jeff, you accomplished more in your 58 years on this earth than most people would in 100 years. But the biggest accomplishment is this LARGE circle of friends and loved ones that have come today to pay tribute to your life." Jeffy's friends, the Hogarths, mused, "We can see the wonder and beauty of your life all around us." Jeff's brother, Brad, thanked Jeff for "all of the many uncomfortable adventures", while Robin's daughter Jenny recalled Jeff spouting her favorite line from "Monty Python and the Holy Grail" Sister-in-law Donna avowed that Jeff's hugs were always the best. His sister, Diane, remarked that Jeff had taken her in his TR3 for her first Big Mac.

Robin's daughter, Shannon, wondered where to turn now for answers to tricky questions. A Thermo coworker, Kurt, said Jeff was a great "soother" on their often-stress-filled daily work talks. A set of neighbors wrote about how Jeff was always working to build his home his own way, and what a wonderful job he had done on it. Some scout parents thanked Jeff for the "unexpected adventures" and called him a "partner in crime".

Neighbor Robin and her husband, of course, constructed a card with a picture of Jeff on the front and a list of the top five reasons Jeff was such a great person:

5. Adept at chasing cats with a garden hose!

4. Great maker of jelly and jam!

3. Excellent builder of room additions!

2. Wine and beer making abilities were superb!

AND THE #1 REASON-

1. He was a wonderful friend and neighbor!

When most of the attendants had departed and it was mostly good neighbors and family my age and younger left, the tone changed. We all knew we could relax and have a drink or several, so we did. The conversation took turns that were alternately silly and somber. My husband's sister began to reveal things none of us had ever suspected in relationship to the Mustang and her adventures therein. We all, in our turn, let our hair down a bit, which was a relief because we all had been pretty tightly wound and driven for days. Gathered in the room Jeff had worked so hard to build, we seemed to come together for a time. Within days I could feel myself separating off from the world, distancing myself from those who wished the best for me.

We all got sick within days, too, with strep throat, the worse case I personally had ever had. Making my way to the clinic a few days after the wake, I marked "widow" on my entrance form, having to do it consciously and for the first time. The doctor, after examining my throat and glands, stated that not only were antibiotics in order, but a shot first, followed by the usual round of pills. He suggesting Keflex, and I agreed, since I had had success with it in the past.

That evening seemed more surreal than even those of the previous week. By the time I got to bed, having left a couple of lights on down the hall, smoke appeared in my vision, but no smoke alarms sounded. Shortly after that, a troop of firefighters, surrounded by flashing lights, charged silently down the hallway towards the back bedroom. Other bizarre visions began, so I decided that I should close my eyes, since the hallucinations were only visual. My dreams that night were also full of fantastic images. I have no idea how strong that antibiotic injection was, but I had never had a reaction like that before. Because I knew right off the bat that this was a result of the drug, I found it all rather amusing.

That bout of illness cost me a few days, as it did for Shauna and Ward. It also made it so I couldn't meet my new grandchild until she was several days old. Jeremie, living in Apple Valley, had given birth to our only granddaughter, Madison. Not long after my visit with her, accompanied by my sister-in-law, Donna, Jeremie wound up having to leave her boyfriend and abandon their home. I was at a meeting at school; Jeremie called the house in a panic, and Jeffy went out to pick up her, the baby, and anything else they could cram into his tiny car. Thus began, right after the upheaval of Jeff's death, a new era for our family.

The course of Jeremie's life had not been smooth ever since we had asked her to leave — twice. So this would be the final test of whether or not we could live together. Luckily, this next year proved to be so very busy for all of us, the rough spots were steamrolled by tasks and jobs most of us had never had to do before. it was a relief to me that Jeremie took on organizing and hiring workers to get the house ready to sell. She cracked the whip when needed and helped keep me on task on days when I wanted to chuck it all. Shauna came down when she could, and absolutely maximized her time there. Ward came along with her at one point, and they were painting fiends. Jeffy worked on things he knew how to do, like dismantle the greenhouse, and took a bit of time to get to know the TR, actually getting it started and off down the street! Well, yes, he also set fire to the garage floor…Ward also came with a friend during Spring break and rebuilt the Mustang well enough to drive it all the way back to Bellingham, WA!

I think every one of us discovered abilities in ourselves we had never known we had. It was a learning time for all.

Over the course of the next several weeks after the wake, I stayed home most of the time, going through paperwork, trying to resolve issues surrounding bank accounts, Social Security, life insurance policies and the like. Now I don't know if most people have a single lockbox or file cabinet in which they keep their stock information, code words, insurance policies and whatnot, but we didn't. We had a safe, three file cabinets, and plenty of flat surfaces in Jeff's part of the inside den, the garage den, and the hobby room to store the three decades-plus accumulation of paperwork. Thing is, older, out-of-date pieces, warranties for appliances we no longer had, insurance policies which had been cashed in or transferred, benefit paperwork for jobs Jeff no longer held, check stubs and paycheck vouchers from a score of years — everything was there. Little had been weeded out and shredded. So this job became twofold — find the important stuff and shred the rest.

I was methodical. I was relentless. I took no prisoners. This effort took weeks, accompanied by shredder downtime, overflowing trashcans out on the street, dozens of Advil for my aching back; I destroyed what I had determined was no longer useful and reorganized the items using a method that made sense to me. We went from four and a half file cabinets to one for me, and one of automotive booklets and small parts for the TR, to be kept in the garage.

I found the stock information, the Schwab account data, life insurance policies (one of them on his workbench in the garage!), what to tell Jeff's last employer, how to calculate his death benefits from two employers (Unocal and Thermo), and a surprise – I had forgotten that he had a policy through my employer as well. So I sent off everything I could find, made all the necessary contacts, and waited.

Jeff's policy was to keep everything. Mine became "Travel Light".

As we got closer to the start of the new school year (Marshall was a year-round school with four staggered start tracks), I started to wonder if I could pull off teaching full-time if I had to get the house ready to sell. I knew the kids and other relatives would help as much as possible, but this dwelling needed work before being put on the market, and all of the physical labor and salesmanship were foreign to me.   However, I would not be able to collect on my pension until I had reached fifty-five and a half years of age. During a grade-level meeting at the end of the school year in June, one of my colleagues, Laurel, revealed that the district had denied the application of a teacher she wanted to partner with due to lack of credentialing, and so she needed a teacher who wanted to work half-time to step into that position. Having been her job sharer many years before when my kids were young, I jumped at the chance. Despite the fact that we were only a little over a week from the start of that track, the school district jammed the paperwork through in time for us to prepare to teach together for my final professional year.

I had felt that this would be the ideal answer to my problem – how to work and yet get the house in shape for being put on the market. Working half-time would continue my benefits, and yet allow me the time to ready myself for retirement, my house for a new owner, and my younger two kids for their decision-making – whether to stay with me and move to Washington or to remain in California and fend for themselves.

In July, school was underway, Laurel and I fell into our familiar pattern of supposedly working half-time, yet knocking ourselves out in order to never be seen as doing too little, and back in Washington Shauna was out for a walk with her dog on the street that extended behind her backyard. She noticed down a driveway of a cluster lot – one where there are two or three houses sharing a driveway and parking area – there was a new home being framed. Upon closer inspection, she could see the approximate size and layout of the home. And she remembered that week between Jeff's death and the wake, having asked me what I needed to come to when I moved to the Bellingham area. "Trees. Just trees. Just enough land cleared for the house to sit on and just trees surrounding it on every side." She *returned to the area with her camera, began clicking away, then went back home to send me the pictures, along with the caption, "Mom, this is your new home."*

My track was off during the month of August to make room for the set of students and teachers who had not yet begun their academic year, and Jeffy's school year at the community college had not yet begun, so we determined that the timing was right for a road trip. We loaded up the Explorer, Jeffy readied some appropriate classic rock CDs, and we set out.

Before we had even left California, I was glad he was on board. We had a flat! Just barely reaching an off-ramp, we hoped not to be rammed by giant trucks as Jeff worked on changing the tire — yet another learning experience because he had never had to do it on that particular car before. Finally, we were again on our way.

One of my favorite memories of that trip involved an electrical storm, eerie sky lighting, and Jimmie Hendrix. We headbanged our way up the 5.

Upon arrival at Shauna's, I contacted a real estate agent and began the work of checking out any and all likely houses within about a half-hour radius of Shauna and Ward's. Some of my search parameters included enough bedrooms in case Jeffy and Jeremie — and Madison, of course — plus, possibly, my mother, decided to come along; a reasonably-sized kitchen, and a new enough house so that I wouldn't be troubled with frequent repairs. After a few days of that it became very clear that Shauna had been right. I put down earnest money on the house down the street behind hers and started discussions with the builder, Lori, who lived on the same street, in terms of some refinements and alterations which would make that house my own.

During each school break I traveled up to Washington to solidify the move up there, buy some furnishings, rugs, and appliances for the house, and check out the area more. I discovered a few furniture stores which held surprising pieces which seemed to go together well in this space. A propane, tile-surround firepit for the upper deck off the living area, some patio furniture to go with it, three differently-shaped wool patterned rugs for the living area, including a long runner to get you from the front door to the greatroom, two loveseats at a right angle taking advantage of the fireplace area, fronted by a square two-level coffee table, a large metal and tile end table, and an interesting little mahogany bookcase they called "hopscotch" which more resembled a tic-tac-toe board, with two deep drawers that fit it perfectly, as well as a refrigerator, washer and dryer, made for a good start for Jeffy's comfort before the rest of the older furniture got up there. (Since we had decided that Jeffy would be moving up there first, with his school year ending in mid-May, it was important to me that he wouldn't have to scramble around setting up the household with no knowledge of what might be needed, even though Shauna and Ward lived just steps away.) I contacted the utilities companies, newspaper subscription services, and started counting the days until our departure for Sudden Valley, Washington.

All of the time I spent during the course of those twelve months after Jeff's death working at my job and the impending retirement, continuing to visit my ailing parents a couple of times a week, getting to know my granddaughter and reinventing my relationships with my kids, preparing the house for sale, making decisions about the new house, and cleaning out every nook and cranny of the old house, all served to occupy my mind and body almost fully. As I entered each room of the old house, I reminded myself of my resolution to eliminate half of everything that was in it — furniture, items in furniture and closets, literally half of the contents of every room. Once you get into the mode of slicing off chunks of your life, it gets a little easier every day. Another reason to achieve this goal was that I knew that the movers would charge by the pound, and that the TR was going to make quite a dent in our moving budget.

It was only when things were quiet, when I was alone, or just after dropping my head onto my pillow, that I could begin to truly deal with what had happened. Mostly, I felt awful for all of the lovely things Jeff was missing out on — retirement, moving to Washington, being with his grandkids, especially the ones he never got to know. He had worked so hard to provide for us all, to build a lasting legacy through stocks and bonds, and had literally built our life in that home, and hadn't lived long enough to "coast". Every night I told him I loved him. And I wondered if I had already exceeded the times I had told him that when he was there to hear it. It was all so unfair to all of us, but mostly for Jeff.

Jeremie, my brother's wife Gloria and I all agreed that Madison seemed to have captured a bit of Jeff's spirit. Often, when she was tiny, she would stare up into the rafters of the family room and smile — at nothing we could see. But it would have made sense that something of Jeff would be floating around amidst his biggest creation. I wished I could participate in what Madison was experiencing. And I hoped Jeff's spirit would decide to accompany us on the move to Washington.

Another huge issue for me during this time was wondering if I had acted on the information that his blood pressure was starting to get to over 140 and more than once, would it have made a difference? Had I nagged, would he have finally gone to the doctor and started on a course of therapy to get his blood pressure back within normal ranges? Had I focused on healthy cooking and dragged him out for walks, would it have mattered? Of course, I will never know the answer…and years later I continue to ask.

Moving away from my parents provided yet another reason to lie there and stew at night. But I had come to believe that the only way to keep my kids from harmful lifestyles was to get out of California.

And me. I needed the trees, clean air and water and liberal atmosphere. I wanted to write this book. Everything about continuing to live in Chino dragged at my spirit. From the moment Jeff died, I started to leave. To separate from stress and repression, the heat and smog. To plan to get my kids out of there. Shauna had known what she was doing, deep inside. She found a better place for her family. In so doing, she revealed one for mine.

Many nights sleep was hard-fought for. A glass or two of wine often helped me at least get to sleep, but rarely maintain it for more than a few hours. Once awake, my mind would race with "what ifs". It was several months before I read information about how alcohol can interfere with one's sleep cycle.

So every other night I switched to ice cream. ;)

With the kids' help, a year after Jeff's death the house was freshly painted inside and out, had new carpet and some new window coverings, the greenhouse was torn down and other yard junk hauled away, the backyard newly landscaped, new sod front and back, a new patio cover over the side yard, and half of everything in the house and garage cleaned out. My brother came and took delivery on the 1960 Chevy truck that had belonged to our dad, Jeremie sold the Jeep during a yard sale, and Ward had driven off the Mustang. We were down to the Ford Explorer and the TR, since Jeff had already finished his school year, driven off to Washington and was in the new house, hosting a couple of his friends there and getting to know the big, beautiful dog Shauna had web-rescued for us.

At that point I started my good-byes to the house. Soon I would no longer see the driveway that was always full of cars, the brick wall under the oak tree where we sat with Jeffy and watched lightning streak across the mountains or flames flicker from the wildfires near Mount Baldy. When would be my last hop over the short wall that separated our property from Robin and Dave's? I wouldn't see the plum crop come in this year, nor the apricots, but that also meant I would no longer be living in The Inland Valley, where the summer temperatures could soar past one hundred and ten, and if it was under 98, the smog would cause you to think there were no mountains nearby. No more autumns of choking gray ash from forest fires. There were certainly SOME things I wouldn't miss!

Walking into the house, I would wonder when the last time would come for me to close that front door. The kitchen we had upgraded, Jeff's amazing double family room with the glowing oak staircase my dog had slid down when the homecleaners accidentally used wax on it, and our bedroom….Well, at least I was taking the bedroom set with me, as well as the old wooden sign that had hung in our bedroom since we married. It read "Familiarity Breeds". Certainly rang true for us.

Saying good-bye to my family had been difficult. I was hoping my parents would be in good enough health so as to be comfortable and not to worry my brother too much. He was still working, living in Riverside, just under an hour away from my parents' house and we had arranged for a caregiver to spend a few hours each day ensuring that my folks were up, having meals and taking their medications. Our preference would have been to get them into assisted living, but they wouldn't hear of it. So while my kids and I were ready for the changes Washington would bring, and I needed to be close to Shauna and her family, there was still the strong pull of family left behind.

Jeff's parents had had a few bouts with illness as well, but at the point I was moving they were doing all right. Plus, they still had two children and several grandchildren in Southern California, and a good support system.

My colleagues staged a lovely retirement party for me and an aide who were leaving the workforce. Skits and silly presents were presented, many using a Star Wars theme, including a large black t-shirt with a sketch of Vader proclaiming that he was framed. My good neighbor and I shed some tears. Some of the school parents declared that I couldn't leave because they still had kids who hadn't gotten to first grade yet. I reminded them of the fantastic first grade team that remained, that they couldn't go wrong with them.

The day school let out (I didn't work the last two days because it was Laurel's turn), I met my students at the park across the street – the same park Jeff had been airlifted from just over a year before – and said my good-byes to them. I had already hugged my co-workers, bid farewell to neighbors. At around five o'clock in the afternoon when the movers finished, we packed our bags and the baby into the car and took off. I knew we wouldn't get all that far in just those few hours, but I was out of there, on my way to a new home and a new life, and I couldn't wait to get started. Jeff rode in the back this time, his ashes resting in the beautiful and unique Native American copper-ensheathed blanket box, and I hoped his spirit rode along with us, too.

Message from The Great Northwest

Jeff would have loved it here. Oh, not Sudden Valley with its codes and restrictions on how you can change the appearance of your house, nor its ban on outbuildings and cars being worked on in full view of the rest of the residents. That's for sure. But he would have adored this area, its cleanliness and purity, the walking trails, the liberalism. He would have happily voted Democrat or Green, knowing that many of his neighbors shared his left-wing leanings. The Farmers' Market and Food Co-Op would have found him a frequent flier. He would have had a flourishing garden, messy but productive, a shop crammed with unfinished projects and obscure tools, a musk ox with dangling hoarfrost stomping in a small pasture. Perhaps he would have bought a small boat and gone down to the lake or ocean to learn to kayak. Cross-country skiing near Mount Baker would have been another year-round pleasure for him.

He would have loved it here and thoroughly enjoyed his retirement. And that is what pains me the most — not for our having lost him, but for what he never got to have. All those years of hard work and savings, and he didn't get to reap the benefits from it. If there is unfairness here, it is less about what the rest of us had to go through and more about what he missed out on.

Jeff was fifty-eight years old when he died of a burst blood vessel in his brain. That tiny malformation, which may have lain dormant and intact for his whole life, finally gave way. While I suppose I should be thankful for the time we had together, for introducing me to some spectacular people in his family, and, especially, for fathering our wonderful children, what saddens me the most is that the time we had was the building and working time, you know? It was the hard part of a marriage, of a family. He did all of the labor and didn't survive to see the fruits of it. So, here I am, in retirement, in a lovely home with a nice view, right down the street from the rest of my family, having the time and energy to write this book. This book about him and what he made. I wanted you, everyone, to know this special, flawed, terrific person I married, and that he was worth the time to get to know. He wouldn't think so, but it's true. And while families all around us, wherever we live, fall apart when people choose the wrong person or decide it's just too hard to make things work, that they are missing out on possibly, probably good things ahead. I would give just about anything to still have my husband here today, despite our having grown apart and found other interests. Had we been given a second chance, we would have never blown it.

But I lost him that tenth night. His last night. And, hundreds of nights later, his family still burns the candle of remembrance and love.

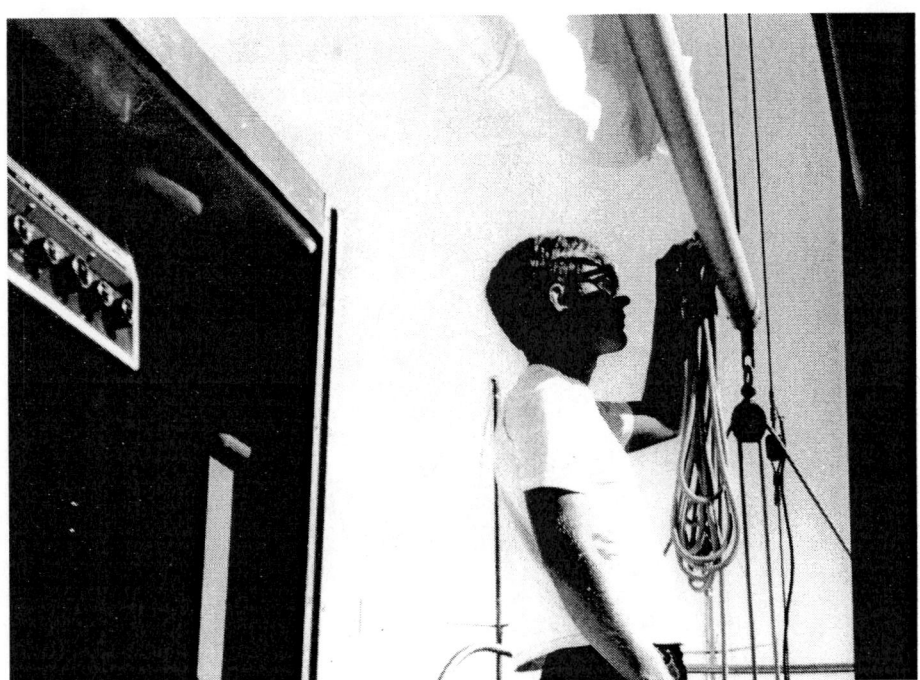

Jeff in his teens on his father's boat.

Sue with Jeremie, Jeff with Shauna, backyard Chino house.

Jeff gathering backpack items for a wintery hike.

Jeff and Brad prepping for Mt. Whitney assault.

Jeff and Sue at Joshua Tree National Monument, late 70s.

Jeff holding oldest grandson Zach at the San Diego Zoo around 2002.

Jeff constructing the Chino house family room.

Claire and Bill Liles, Sue's parents.

Sue's brother Bill Liles and his wife Gloria.

Sue and Jeff's daughter Jeremie with neighbor Robin Emery.

The Parsons clan at the Chino house, Thanksgiving 2003.

Our granddaughter, Madison.

Jeff on the bridge overlooking Whatcom Creek, Bellingham, WA.

Sue and Jeff, 2002.